Chapel Time

With Teens - For Parents

Published by Mindstir Media, LLC
45 Lafayette Rd | Suite 181| North Hampton, NH 03862 | USA
1.800.767.0531 | www.mindstirmedia.com

Printed in the United States of America
ISBN-13: 978-1-7332346-2-7
Library of Congress Control Number: 2019908164

Chapel Time

With Teens - For Parents

Bill Spanjer III

53 Condensed Devotional And Theological Chapel Talks

MINDSTIR MEDIA

- *Dedications* -

To My Daughter, Kristy,

an angel sent from God to save my life.

Without her love, dedication, loyalty and determination,

my dreams of service to our Lord, Jesus Christ,

would have ended in November 2016.

With her patience, wise nursing care and enduring affection,

I am able to fulfill my dreams for Him.

Thank you, Lord.

– *Acknowledgments and Thanks* –

To my God, Lord and Savior, Jesus Christ

To my daughter, Kristy, who not only typed this book but corrected all of my many faux pas

To my wife, Kathleen, who worked on this manuscript in spite of her grueling teaching schedule

To my publisher, J.J. Hebert of MindStir Media, who graciously decided to take another chance on me

To my son, Tim, who designed my book jacket, and his wife, Vaughan for producing the wonderful illustrations

To my grandson, Andy, who is a genius on the computer and whose great knowledge and skill made my task much easier.

To all of my wonderful students who, over the decades, taught me how to love them and this ministry, and whom I had the privilege of coaching, teaching and administrating over. Now the mantle rests on them to further learn and pray that God will give them an obsession for Him, for the Gospel of Jesus Christ and for the ministry to which He calls them.

And finally, special thanks to my teachers and theological mentors:

Professor "Pop" Suplee,
Professor "Buck" Hatch,
Dr. George Cannon,
and especially, Dr. R.C. Sproul

FOREWORD

We live in a day of diminishing interest in living a godly life. Too many of our precious young people are distracted by the shallow offerings of immediate gratification and the too often distasteful, non-meaningful menu of a watered-down form of godliness. The result is that they drift further and further away from the true moorings of God's message for a life that is well-lived in Jesus. Within the pages of this collection of chapel messages are found not only words that have biblical derivation but require spiritual application. What reverberates off the pages of this book is passion, persuasion, and prophetic implications. In other words, these writings are not a light dusting of the profound truths of God's Word. With both relevance and scriptural rigor, the Coach touches on those issues that our young are dealing with today. What makes this devotional book so valuable is that its author has lived and interacted with young people, through the means of Christian education, for most of his life. And out of this life-long experience, he has set to print that which can set fire to the heart of the young and old alike to be all they can be for the Kingdom of God.

Dr. Sandy M. Outlar
Ambassador to Christian Schools
Lancaster Bible College,
Lancaster, Pennsylvania

TABLE OF CONTENTS

INTRODUCTION

I want to explain what you are about to read. When we first opened our Christian school in 1986, as part of the class schedule, I wanted to have a chapel first thing in the morning. I planned a half hour to do this, from 8:00 to 8:30. After opening exercises, a scripture reading and announcements, I had about twenty minutes to bring a short message. After a few months, certain faculty members suggested to me at a staff meeting that these chapels were taking too much time out of the class schedule. They wanted me to do chapel one day a week, taking about thirty minutes. They reasoned, by taking five minutes off each period that day we could get a full chapel time in every week. I thought that that was a good idea, but I wanted to send my students off to class first thing every day with a challenge from the Lord. I thought of the words of the psalmist,

> *O God, thou art my God; early will I seek thee: my soul thirsteth for thee, my flesh longeth for thee in a dry and thirsty land, where no water is*
> *(Psalm 63:1).*

I thought, if ever we lived in a dry, thirsty land wherein no relief is, it is today in our culture. So, I worked out a compromise with my faculty. I would do a fifteen-minute chapel—five minutes for opening exercises and announcements and then a five to ten-minute chapel talk with a brief truth theme at the end, which I hoped would stick with them all day. That's what we did for over thirty years and counting. I found pastors, missionaries, laymen and women in ministries and other faculty to do Mondays and Tuesdays. Wednesdays, class officers did chapel. I did it every Thursday, and on Fridays we had prayer groups. I accumulated over 900 short chapel talks given to my students and have included fifty-two plus one in this little book.

But first I want to tell the reader about our student body. About one-third of them had given no serious thought to their need of salvation. They were too busy enjoying the norms of our Christian culture. They had not had the demands of the gospel brought clearly to their attention. About another one-third of our students had professed to be Christian but had not taken their commitment seriously. The final one-third were very committed to their Christian faith. Most, but not all, came from strong Christian families, belonged to their church youth group, were involved in the school's Youth Conquest with Christ community service programs, and went on short mission trips.

This was a diverse group to challenge every morning. This diversity of spirituality brought considerable criticism from our evangelical community. "Why don't you have a requirement that only Christian kids can come to your school?" Another person once complained, "You're just trying to get more money at the expense of our children." After these overwhelming complaints, I started accepting only kids from church families.

However, I changed my mind early on when a female student came to me pleading, "Please accept Beth. I know she is not a Christian, but she has been attending my youth group, and she wants to get out of the public school and into a Christian environment." So, I interviewed her. I knew my parents wanted only kids from Christian families admitted to the school. My dilemma was that some of my worst-behaved students in school came from "Christian" families. They were not good examples to the rest of the students. Most of my non-Christian kids who took their studies and behavior seriously were a pleasure to have.

Further, I saw my obligation before the Lord was to teach and preach the gospel to all kids that God sent to me, making disciples of all, if possible. By accepting kids that demonstrated that they were serious about understanding their faith (Christianity) and serious about their behavior, I solved my dilemma. But first I had to implement the "Two Strikes, You're Out" policy—one serious misbehavior, one second chance if the student was genuinely sorry and wrote letters of apology to his teachers and fellow students he offended. Another serious event, that's two strikes, you're out.

The families of the Christian community were happy because they knew that their student did not have negative influences around them. And as a school, we could fulfill our mission to evangelize and disciple all who registered.

Because of our new policy, many positive things happened. We had a church attendance requirement for all our students. Several non-churched families decided to accompany their student to church, some became Christians and joined the church! One father, in particular, several years later, became an elder in his church!

Anyway, these were the diverse students we had in chapel every day and for whom I had to prepare a message for every week. I needed "A Thought for Today," well-illustrated, down-to-earth, theologically correct, ending with a "truth theme" that would be easy to remember. I hoped this would stay in their minds all day. I also hoped my experiences in high school, in the military as a Marine, as a flight instructor, businessman and farmer would help in this endeavor. I particularly designed the subjects so that parents might go over them with their student later. That would help them support their family values and provide a spiritual truth for them.

My goal at **Chapel Time** was to reinforce the gospel, its

centrality, and claims on the lives of young people, this from a Reformation perspective. My prayer for all readers of this short book is that they wouldn't be diverted by their friends, their culture, self-efforts, or anything that would lead away from the gospel of grace offered by our Lord Jesus Christ. But put all their trust, energy, and faith in Him alone for salvation from the dreadful consequences of sin. I trust every student reading this book will be devoted to the infallible word of God and live their lives always "In His Presence, Under His Authority, and For His Glory—*Coram Deo.*"

CHAPEL TALK

I

Love Our Enemies?!

"Ye have heard that it hath been said, Thou shalt love thy neighbour, and hate thine enemy. But I say unto you, Love your enemies, bless them that curse you, do good to them that hate you, and pray for them which despitefully use you, and persecute you."

Matthew 5:43-44

LOVE OUR ENEMIES?!

Background: I had a girl come to me crying one afternoon. She told me about a "mean girl" incident where another girl in school said very vile things about her on the internet. She showed me the comments. She said, "I hate her." I replied, "I understand how you feel but hating someone will only be bad for you." Then I counseled her with scripture. After that, I confronted the girl in question. She apologized and agreed to take down the post, but I had to suspend her for two days from school regardless. I talked to my assistant principal, and she said that there was a lot of that going on in school, so I decided to do a chapel on the subject.

Today's thought is, "Do you love your enemies?" I believe one of the hardest sayings of Jesus is found in Matthew 5:44. "But I say unto you, love your enemies, bless them that curse you, do good to them that hate you, and pray for them which despitefully use you and persecute you." I want to tell you a short story.

On May 8, 1945, our nation declared victory in Europe (V-E Day). Now the military could shift its efforts to the second front, the defeat of Japan in the South Pacific. The U.S. had three great fighter planes that helped defeat the Germans in the air war. Most popular was the North American P-51. It was sleek, fast, and ruled the skies over Europe. Next was the P-38. It was a twin-engine super-fighter. It had a twin tail behind each engine locked together with a horizontal stabilizer. It was known as the "Forked Devil" by the enemy. And thirdly, there was the P-47D Thunderbolt. It was the largest of the three, was powered by a Pratt and Whitney 18-cylinder twin-row R2800 engine—the same engine that was in the famous Navy and Marine fighter that flew off the aircraft carriers—the F4U Corsair.

I am telling you these facts because the P-47D ended up in the hands of the 460th Fighter Squadron attached to the 348th Fighter Group. One was piloted by Major Bill Durham. He was the wingman for Colonel Ted Kearby, Bill's best friend. Now, a wingman's job is to protect the other when one pilot engages an enemy plane. On March 6, 1944, Kearby and Durham were on patrol near Wewar off the New Guinea coast. Kearby spotted a Japanese bomber and began an attack, shooting the bomber down, but while he was circling the downed plane (which was a big mistake), a KI-43 Oscar racked Kearby's Thunderbolt with machine gun fire. Durham got on the tail of the Oscar and shot it down. He then lost sight of Kearby's plane. Another pilot said he saw Kearby bail out and his parachute open. Durham lingered but could not find Kearby. Knowing that Japanese pilots would often fire upon American pilots hanging from their parachutes, Durham became frantic to find his best friend. Running low on fuel, Durham had no other choice than to return to his airfield. Sure enough, a search party on New Guinea later found Col. Kearby's body hanging from his parachute in a palm tree, riddled with machine gun bullets. Durham was devastated.

Several months later while on patrol, Durham downed another Oscar. Circling, he watched the Japanese pilot bail out. As he circled, he thought of Col. Kearby; now he could get revenge. As he had the Japanese pilot in his gun sights, he recalled later, "that it was as if the Lord put his hand on my shoulder and said, 'Bill, don't do it.'" (*Aviation History Magazine*, May 2008, "Uncommon Chivalry"). As Durham watched the pilot parachute into the ocean, he noticed that the Japanese pilot had no life jacket. Now, Japanese pilots were totally expendable; they had no survival gear. U.S. pilots, on the other hand, had on them a Mae West life vest, a one-man inflatable life raft, a fifteen-day supply of food, shark repellant, a knife, fishing gear, and a mirror to reflect the sunlight in the eyes of pilots passing overhead.

But this Japanese pilot had nothing and could only tread water for a few minutes. So, Durham took off his own life vest, made a low pass, and threw it out of his cockpit to the downed Oscar pilot. This left Durham without protection for his long flight back to base.

Bill Durham, in his P-47,
giving Japanese pilot his Mae West
(note: markings from D-Day invasion remain on his plane)

So, you hate someone just because they called you vile names? How about if they killed your best friend who was help-less? Hate does no one any good. And where did Durham get this idea anyway? He got it in church and his high school where the scriptures were read every day (as they were in most schools and as it was in mine). He got it from Christian values that per-meated our culture in the 1940s and 1950s and now in schools like ours. Major Durham is an example of true Christian virtue. "Love your enemies, bless them that curse you, do good to them that hate you." Why does Jesus say this? "That you may be the children of your Father which is in heaven." What kind of Father is He? He's the One who loves His enemies... you and me! When we were enemies (of God), we were reconciled to God by the death of His Son (Romans 5:10). Even if others say vile things about you, be like your heavenly Father.

Closing Prayer:

Lord, we may not have the courage to resist evil the way Major Durham did, but keep us from overre-acting to trivial insults. We know that the greatest insult was laid upon You at the crucifixion and You said, "Forgive them because they know not what they are doing." Help this to be our prayer also. Please deliver us from evil. Amen.

Truth Theme: Remember God's words to Bill Durham: "Bill, don't do this." Hate will destroy you; love will heal you. Be chil-dren of your heavenly Father.

coach@chapelfield.org

CHAPEL TALK
2

Can You Win "Hands Down"?

"I press toward the mark for the prize of the high calling of God in Christ Jesus."

Philippians 3:14

A Thought for Today

CAN YOU WIN "HANDS DOWN"?

Confidence is a very big factor in success. Winning athletes rarely say, "I had no confidence that I could win." Most of the time they say, "I had great confidence I could do this." The word confidence means *trust*, but what's an athlete or any other successful person trust in? He may trust in his or her ability. Certainly, you have to have the ability to compete. You may trust your training or your coaches. All successful people, whether it be in sports, business, farming, academics, or anything else, have to train, study and practice. That's what you are doing at Chapel Field right now—studying and training so that you can have the confidence to take it to the next level.

But there is one other factor in the ultimate trust that you need to get over the finish line. Some call it guts, some call it an adrenaline rush and others, the extra oomph. Mike Tyson, the famous boxer, once said, "When I see victory in sight, I give it the go and finish him off." It's that extra "go" at the last minute that gives all great athletes the victory. It's like a full-court press even when you are ahead in the game, to complete the victory.

I don't know if you have ever heard the expression, "He won hands down." I want to tell you, if you want to be successful in life, or in your Christian life, or do great things for your Lord, you have to win hands down. When a jockey and his horse are approaching the finish line, and the competition is closing in, instead of holding his reins between his thumb and forefinger, he lets the reins fall by turning his hands down, thereby giving his steed the signal to go all-out, to muster all the adrenaline and oomph he has to win the race.

Bill Spanjer III   11

Racing towards the finish line

We don't know how close the finish line may be, but we have to run like it may be tomorrow. The Bible tells us that we can't get that extra oomph—the go—to complete our Christian calling by our own extra oomph. We can't count on our own training or our abilities, although they are very important. Out ultimate trust, confidence, and endurance must be in our Lord, God Himself. We must go all-out, hands down, in His service. Why? Because that's what He did for us at Calvary. Jacob did it when he fought with the angel at Jabbok. Moses did at the Red Sea. David did it in his battle with Goliath. The apostle Paul did it when he pressed on to the mark of his high calling in Christ. Martin Luther did it in his victory to save the gospel of salvation by grace through faith alone at the Diet of Worms. They all let it all out, hands down for the Lord Jesus. Why? Because He is the author and finisher of our faith, who for the prize that was set before Him endured the cross (Hebrews 12:1-2b, AMP).

Give it your all, hands down! Put the pedal to the metal, give it oomph! You can finish a winner and have trophies to lay at His feet in the end.

Closing Prayer:

Lord, forgive us for settling on coming in the back of the pack. Challenge us and inspire us to endure with confidence and trust in You in the race You have set before us that we may rejoice with You on that great day when we will all stand before You for You to judge our effort in the race of life. Amen.

Truth Theme: In Christ, we will not be judged for our failures but judged for our courage, endurance, and enthusiasm for Him and His mission.

coach@chapelfield.org

CHAPEL TALK

3

Are You Profitable?

*Profit lies not in what you are required
to do but in what's done beyond what
you are required to do.*

Based on Luke 17:7-10

ARE YOU PROFITABLE?

Text for today–Luke 17:10:

So likewise, ye, when ye shall have done all those things which are commanded you, say, we are unprofitable servants. We have done that which was our duty to do.

I don't know about you, but I grew up in a home where my father had all kinds of sayings: "If a job is worth doing, it's worth doing right," "If you start something, finish it," and so it goes. But one saying he pounded into my head was, "Fifteen minutes early, fifteen minutes late." What he meant by that was, whenever you work for someone, show up fifteen minutes early and after your pay time is over, do another fifteen minutes working at your job. It will get you big rewards. He taught me, always do the extra, don't go with the crowd (groupthink) and don't always play it safe. These three "d's" stayed with me all my life.

It was a very short time after that we all got notices to join a branch of the service, or we would get drafted into the army. So, some friends and I decided to join the Marine Corps. There wasn't much opportunity to put my dad's principles into play in Parris Island because we got up at 5:30, did training all day and lights out was 10:00 p.m. But Sea School was another great opportunity. There we got up at 6:30 a.m., had breakfast and were in class until 4:00 p.m. So, I got to class at 7:40, straightened the desks and got my notebook up to date. After class, I stayed for about fifteen minutes to clean up the classroom and then I left.

All my classmates would change into their "greens" and go to the bars on East Main Street in Norfolk. I did not like to go with the crowd, so I spotted an obstacle course right across from my barracks. I ran it forward and backward every day at 4:40. I felt good about getting the exercise. On graduation day, we got our certificates and ship assignments. I was excited anticipating on which ship I would spend the next three years. Would it be the aircraft carrier, the *USS Forrestal,* or perhaps the battleship, *USS New Jersey*? When my name was finally called, the Marine colonel said, "Spanjer—Com Cru, Div Six." What?! I thought, why not a ship? Did I get a rowboat or something? I asked an instructor standing near my seat. "What ship did I get?" He said, "You are attached to the Commander Cruiser Division Six. You're an admiral's orderly, driver, assistant, and security. You'll be on all kinds of ships." Wow!

The admiral I worked for was Rear Admiral Lawrence R. Daspit, a truly great man. I received an open gangway pass, meaning I could go and come off the ship at any time. I got on guided missile cruisers, aircraft carriers, drove the admiral all around England, Spain, and Italy, and best of all, I answered only to the admiral. No Marine or any officer had control over me. I had the best job an enlisted man in the service could get.

A shipmate asked me, "How did you get this job?" My mind went back to graduation day. I said, "I said goodbye to my instructors and the sergeant major. I asked him, 'How did I get this assignment?' He said, 'Your instructors told me you always came to class early and eager to learn and my office was located right across from the obstacle course. I saw you run it every afternoon, rain or shine, while your buddies were hanging out in bars in Norfolk. I had one top assignment, and I gave it to you.'" Wow! My father's advice paid off big-time.

Jesus said that when you do all your requirements, you are

still unprofitable. The extra then is profit. You think that when you go to church, youth group and get good grades in a Christian school that you should be complimented? That's what you're supposed to do. Good grades are what you are commanded to get! However, when you go out and hand out tracts, or you visit an old folks' home to pray and read scripture to them on your free time, that's doing the extra. When you get on a short-term missions trip to help the needy on your vacation time, that's the extra. Then you are a profitable servant.

Why do we do this? Because Jesus did the extra for us? He went to the cross. He didn't do what the group wanted. He didn't play it safe. He died that we might live! Do the extra. Go beyond your requirements (what's commanded of you) and great will be your reward now and in heaven.

Closing Prayer:

Lord, give us eyes to see, ears to hear and minds to understand what You are speaking to us, that we might accomplish Your commands and do exceedingly above what we are required to do, to be profitable servants unto You. Amen.

Truth Theme: Yogi Berra said, "It's not over till it's over." It's over when you have given your life to Jesus. That's the extra He wants.

coach@chapelfield.org

CHAPEL TALK

4

How Short is Your Fuse?

(Part I)

*"Wherefore, my beloved brethren,
let every man be swift to hear,
slow to speak, slow to wrath."*

James 1:19

HOW SHORT IS YOUR FUSE? (Part I)

Kids, dogs are wonderful creatures. They are called man's best friend. They are loyal and don't judge you. They just love you. They are used by police for sniffing out drugs or tracking down criminals, and even for searching for missing children. But also, dogs are much maligned in our culture. We have many negative expressions related to dogs: "He's mad as a dog." "He lies like a dog." Even in World War II, soldiers were called "dog faces."

However, I believe the worst dog-related expression ever used was when Jesus referred to a Canaanite woman as a dog. Why did He say that? What provoked Jesus to use so harsh a description? Let's read the text together. Turn in your Bibles to Matthew 15:21-28:

> Then Jesus went *thence,* and departed into the coasts of Tyre and Sidon. And, behold, a woman of Canaan came out of the same coasts, and cried unto him, saying, 'Have mercy on me, O Lord, thou son of David; my daughter is grievously vexed with a devil.' But he answered her not a word. And his disciples came and besought him, saying, 'Send her away; for she crieth after us.' But he answered and said, 'I am not sent but unto the lost sheep of the house of Israel.' Then came she and worshiped him, saying, 'Lord, help me.' But he answered and said, 'It is not meet to take the children's bread, and to cast it to dogs.' And she said, 'True, Lord: yet the dogs eat of the crumbs which fall from their masters' table.' Then Jesus answered and said unto her,

'O woman, great is thy faith: be it unto thee even as thou wilt.' And her daughter was made whole from that very hour.

Several commentators have expressed the opinion that Jesus was testing this woman. Others have said that since Jesus later granted her request that He changed His mind. I don't believe either of these explanations is true. Since Jesus knew already what this woman's response would be, I think Jesus wanted to demonstrate to His disciples who wanted to chase her away, how long a fuse she had before she got mad or just walked away. The message here is if we are to have great faith, we must have great humility and great perseverance. "Yes, I am a dog." Great humility. "But even the dogs get the crumbs from the master's table." Great perseverance!

Bomb with short fuse

Please note, kids, she prefaced her remarks by acknowledging Jesus as the Messiah (Son of David) claiming He was Lord and that He spoke the truth. Kids, do you want a miracle in your life? Worship Jesus as Lord of your life, Author of all truth and serve Him with great humility and great perseverance. You will receive blessings upon blessings.

Closing Prayer:

Oh Lord, we confess that we have a very short fuse. We revolt at the slightest criticism. We often react in anger and bitterness, thus self-rejecting your benefits. Please give us the confession, the humility, and the perseverance of this Canaanite woman that we may live with You for all eternity. Amen.

Truth Theme: Remember, whenever you have overwhelming problems and difficulties in the future, confess who Jesus is, have confidence in His ability to overcome them and praise Him relentlessly.

coach@chapelfield.org

CHAPEL TALK

5

How Short is Your Fuse?

(Part II)

"... constantly rejoicing in hope...
steadfast and patient in distress."

Romans 12:12, AMP

HOW SHORT IS YOUR FUSE? (Part II)

Last week I talked to you about the pagan Canaanite woman who put to shame the faith of not only Jesus's disciples and all of Israel, but she bore the insult of being called a dog. She was shunned by Jesus's disciples. "Send her away!" they said. "Her crying and crying is bothering us!"

However, her cries for mercy, her confession that Jesus was the Messiah and Lord, her humility and perseverance finally got to Jesus. He used this woman's great faith as a teaching moment for His disciples. This Canaanite woman had a very long fuse. If I were called a pagan and a dog, I fear that I would react much differently.

Bomb with long fuse

I used this strategy of Jesus's as a principal early on in our school years to find out whether a student with a major behavior problem could muster up the kind of courage exhibited by the Canaanite woman. I had two students who were both bullies— disruptive and disrespectful to teachers. One of them also used very bad language. Unable to see any effort to change, I had held student/parent conferences with both families the prior month, but to no avail. Finally, before I dismissed the boys from school, I had one last meeting with them in my office. The first one was David Martin. He came into the room and sat down on the chair in front of my desk. I rehearsed his unacceptable behavior with him from our detention list. "Davy," I said, "you are the worst kid I ever had in school; you are acting like a depraved dog. You need to be put over your father's knee and whipped."

I waited for his reaction. And I didn't have to wait long. He gritted his teeth, his face got red, and his eyes narrowed in anger. I thought he was going to come across my desk and hit me. His actions justified every claim I had made against him. And he had an excuse for everything. Bullying? "I was just kidding around." Language? "The teacher didn't hear me right!" Disrespect? "The teacher disrespected me!" And so it went. I told him that I loved him in spite of his actions, but that his behavior could not be tolerated in our school. There was no remorse, no apology, no acknowledgment that he had done anything wrong. So, I called his parents and said, "I am very sorry. I gave Davy a second chance after our parent conference, but his behavior has gotten worse, and he shows no remorse. You will have to transfer him." Then I called Donnie Mackay.

I reviewed his negative behaviors. I told him what I had told Davy. Then I said to Donnie, "You are a disrespectful bully, and a poor representative of your family and your God. Your father should take you out behind the barn and give you a good whooping" Just as I had with Davy, I waited for a reaction. It came quickly. Tears filled his eyes, and he said sadly, "I didn't know you felt that way about me. Am I really that bad?"

"Worse," I said. He put his face in his hands and sobbed. "I am so sorry, Coach. Please don't kick me out. What do I have to do to make this right?"

I said, "Donnie, you are going to have to make a public apology to the teachers and the student body." He nodded in agreement. I gave him chapel time the next day, and he told the faculty, the staff, and the whole student body how he had let them down, and how sorry he was. He concluded by promising that he would be a better example and asking them to forgive him. Wow! What a tough thing to do in front of your peers. I had never seen that level of courage in a teen before.

Kids, it is clear that Davy had a very short fuse and it led him to end his time at Chapel Field in disgrace. Donnie, on the other hand, had a lengthy fuse and it ended, finally, in his graduation from Chapel Field, with honors! He was a hero among our faculty and a Christ-like example to our students. A Christ-like figure who follows Jesus. The Canaanite woman and Donnie each had a true confession that came from humility and perseverance. How short is your fuse? Jesus himself reminds us in Matthew 5:5 that, "Blessed are the meek, for they shall inherit the earth" (ASV). They will have a long fuse.

Closing Prayer

Oh, Lord, how often do we get uptight and resentful about criticism and destroy ourselves in the end? Lord, give us long fuses, time to consider what our correct reaction should be. Give us, we ask, humility and perseverance to do the right thing. Amen.

Truth Theme: Remember, humility and perseverance are attributes of God. Be ye like Him.

coach@chapelfield.org

CHAPEL TALK

6

Is Jesus Really a Wimp as Portrayed?

"Jesus, a righteous Indiana Jones, who drove money changers from the sanctuary with the sting of His whip, a man's man was He."

Author

IS JESUS REALLY A WIMP AS PORTRAYED?

*Background: There was a discussion in school
that Jesus is depicted in movies and pictures as a
milquetoast character. This was my answer:*

Good morning, students! We only have a short time this morning for chapel, so I want to talk with you briefly about how Jesus is misrepresented in our culture. In *The Quest for the Historical Jesus*, 19th-century writer Albert Schweitzer influenced by David Strauss's *Life of Jesus,* concluded that Jesus was an idealist—a noble example but wholly human. They portrayed an untouchable Jesus surrounded by myth and fable who sought to build the Kingdom of God, but who in the end, was a failure, dying in confusion and frustration. Half of Western Christendom has bought *this* Jesus.

When the 20th-century media got done with Jesus, it left us with a wimp. In George Stevens's *The Greatest Story Ever Told*, a slender, frail Jesus quietly slips through the Judean countryside, subject to His circumstances, at the mercy of men, meekly on the way to His destiny where He softly whispers, "It is finished." Sweet Jesus, meek and mild, is the great evangelical distortion.

Kids, as we race out of the 20th century, a new Jesus is being presented—the Cosmic Jesus! The New Age does not want to be left out. The Cosmic Jesus is that Christ spirit that is in all of us—and in animals, in stars, in rocks! Ha, finally a connection between Christianity and paganism! The cycle is completed. We can worship the creation rather than the creator and do it in the name of Christ. Now as we move into the 21st century, Jesus is a distorter according to the neo-modernist. After all, Jesus, you know there's really no ultimate truth.

"Hollywood" Jesus

But will the real Jesus please stand up? Surprise! He's not the historical Jesus of Schweitzer. He's not the milquetoast weakling made in the USA, nor is He the cosmic spirit. He is the biblical Jesus. He's the God-man who controls nature with the sound of His voice. Storms stop. The lame walk. Dead rise. He's the forgiver of sins! He's God! He died on the cross, conquered death and lives again. He is a man's man. A true righteous Indiana Jones, who drove profiteers from the sanctuary with the sting of a whip. He blasted hypocrites, liars, and distorters of the truth. "You're whitewashed tombs! You're dead men's bones." He criticized an obstinate follower, "Get behind Me, Satan." Subject to no man or circumstance was He. "No man takes my life. I have the power to lay it down; I have the power to take it up again." He was compassionate to women, children, and the unsophisticated sinner. He forgave those who did not know what they did but yelled from the cross for all writers to hear, "It is finished!" as He was about to pay for the sins of the believing world.

No wimp is He, no cosmic spirit either. Real, alive, wholly God, wholly human—the Way, the Truth, and the Life. The ultimate hero for every boy, girl, man, and woman. The sanctified sultan of swat! He came into the world He created like a lamb. He roared like a lion. He will storm back with justice and vengeance, and with salvation for believers. Kids, that is the *biblical* Jesus.

Closing Prayer:

Dear Lord, Isaiah the prophet wrote, "he hath no form or comeliness; and when we see him, there is no beauty that we should desire him." Though the world has a distorted view of Jesus, we know our Lord was compassionate yet authoritative, loving yet commanding—a man's man. Help us to represent Him as He is. Amen.

Truth Theme: Be proud of the biblical Jesus. He was rugged and strong yet loving and caring, the Truth, an example for every man, woman, and child.

coach@chapelfield.org

CHAPEL TALK
7
There's Too Much to Remember!

"Remember is an action word"

Based on Ecclesiastes 12:1

THERE'S TOO MUCH TO REMEMBER!

Kids, remembering could save your life—and your *eternal* life. Our scripture for this morning is Luke 22:19: *"Do this in remembrance of me."*

For about fifteen years, I had a banner in front of our chapel that said, "I don't expect you to be who you are, but I expect you to be better than who you are." I got this saying from my dad when I was in school growing up. Each night when we were having dinner my dad would ask us kids what we did in school that day. We would go around and say what we did and what grade we got on our recent tests. When we were done, my dad would say to each of us, "That's good. Do it better the next time." That thought stayed with me when I studied. I would try to get better grades and improve my basketball skills. I can remember once I had received a seventy-five on a test. The next time I took a test from that teacher I got the same grade. I went to that teacher after class and begged her to give me one point more on that test so I could tell my father I did better that time.

We know we can all strive to do better in every aspect of our lives. The apostle Peter reminds us, "In your faith supply moral excellence, in your moral excellence, knowledge" (2 Peter 1:5, NAS).

I thought this saying would encourage students to seek to do better in every aspect of life. I've used this motto almost every day of my life, in studies, in sports, in business, and in ministry. It taught me not only to do things better the second time but also not to make the same mistake twice! This was a big-time rule for me. However, certain staff members criticized the motto saying it sounded too much like an order, rather than an encouragement. I didn't agree, but I sought a change. The verse I came up with, you can see behind me, is "Remember now thy Creator in the days of thy youth" (Ecclesiastes 12:1).

I chose that verse for two reasons. First, it is a reminder to you to seek God while you are young. As the cares of this world become greater and greater, you will become distracted from His imperatives for you. Secondly, I chose this verse because remembering is an action word, just like my father's motto to me meant taking action to do it better the next time I did it. And also remembering Pearl Harbor was a call to action that rallied us to victory in World War II and remembering 9-11 was a call to action against the Taliban, ISIS and all Islamic terrorists.

So, what did Jesus mean, Do this in remembrance of Me? We know He was speaking of taking communion in our church. But what does He want us to remember that He did? When we remember someone, we think of the most unusual thing about them. For example, at a recent class reunion, someone said, "Where's Louie?" We all had a good laugh remembering Louie and when Ricky bet Louie $10 he wouldn't kiss Miss Jones in front of our English Lit class. He did it, and we were still talking about it sixty years later (you can read about this episode in my book, *The Obstacle Course*).

Sometimes remembering events can bring good times; sometimes not remembering can be tragic. Now brace yourselves. I am going to tell you another aviation story about a good friend from my flying days, Erik Uhnjem (pronounced, "onion"). I met Erik through aviation. He was a graphic artist and designed all our logos at our fellowship, Chapel Field, Youth Conquest, Matthew 25, and Dwaarkill Study Center. Erik and his wife Jane, after learning to fly, bought a small airplane and loved to fly locally on weekends. They soon wanted to get a more sophisticated 4-seat airplane to take friends and fly to more distant places. They found one for sale in northern Connecticut. So, one Sunday, they took off in their little plane to look at it and take a demonstration flight. The owner met them at the airport. However, the owner, in his pre-flight check, forgot to fully put in the fuel cut-off knob. Now, kids, an airplane does not shut off like a car. In a car, you simply turn off the key. But an airplane must be shut off by pulling the fuel cut-off knob out. This is so all the remaining fuel in the engine gets burned up. Any remaining fuel would eat away at the engine parts. As part of a pre-flight checklist, the pilot must check that knob to make sure it is full in so the airplane will get full power when taking off. The airplane owner forgot to check this knob. It remained about halfway out. This was just enough to get the plane up but not enough to keep it flying, so after takeoff, they didn't have enough power, and they crashed in the middle of a housing development. The pilot and Jane were killed, and Erik spent a year in the hospital recovering from his injuries. He lost everything just because the pilot didn't remember to put that knob in.

In taking communion, Jesus said, "Do this in remembrance of me." When we talk about remembering Jesus, the first thought that comes to mind is His sacrifice on the cross to save us from the consequences of our sins. So, we must take action on what He accomplished for us—repent, believe, trust, and serve Him. Have you done that? That would be our action to do in remembering Him, just like Pearl Harbor or 9-11.

Kids, why am I telling you these tragic stories about Erik's deadly plane crash and Christ's cruel death on the cross? Because remembering your mistakes and doing better the next time will save your life. In life, if you want to get to your destination safely, keep your mixture full in. You will need all the power you can get. If you want to get safely to eternal life, make sure you follow your pre-flight checklist. It's right there in the gospels. Remembering is an action word.

Closing Prayer:

Oh, heavenly Father, forgive us for not taking action in our remembrance of You. You have asked us to live lives of repentance, holiness, and service. Forgive us when we fail. Challenge us and inspire us to live lives that please You and allow us to fly safely home to be with You for eternity. Amen.

Truth Theme: All truth demands a positive action from you. In the physical and material world, obeying the rules will save your life. Obeying God's truth in Jesus will save your *eternal* life. Is that too much to remember?

coach@chapelfield.org

CHAPEL TALK
8

Are You an Underdog?

"True Christians may be the underdogs of this world, but they are the underdogs that race to victory, overcoming this world. "

Author

ARE YOU AN UNDERDOG?

Kids, the answer is yes. The word *underdog* comes from the dog-racing sport in England in the mid-1900s. It seems that English breeds were the best dogs for racing. When Australia wanted to get in the dog-racing competition, it sent their dogs to England to compete. These dogs were not the same caliber as the British racing dogs.

Consequently, the odds were often 10-to-1 against the Aussie dogs. In other words, if you bet one pound (the English equivalent to the dollar) and the Aussie dog won, you would get ten pounds back! But Australian dogs would rarely win. That's why the odds were so great against them. Australia was known as the country Down Under. Hence, their dogs were called *underdogs*.

Racing dogs

Kids, in my life, I always found myself rooting for the underdogs. Joe Lewis, the Brown Bomber, was a black boxer and was not supposed to win the World's Championship. Jackie Robinson faced a similar judgment. "Play in the Majors? Not a chance." The Tuskegee Airmen, known as the Red Tails for the red paint on the vertical stabilizers on their P-51s, who fought above Europe in World War II, were judged not smart enough to fly fighter planes. But I rooted for them, and they turned out to be one of the most decorated squadrons in the war.

If you are a child of God, a Christian, you too are an underdog. Just think of Gideon for example. He went against 10,000 Philistines with 300 men. What do you think the odds were for Gideon's success? 50-to-1? 10,000-to-3? If that were the case and you placed a $1.00 bet on Gideon, you would win $10,000. But no one bets on a dog or a person with those kinds of odds against them.

What are the odds against you as a Christian? Odds are figured by mathematical possibilities of success. What are the odds that you wouldn't ever lie again, or lust again, or covet again, or get mad at your father or any other person? The odds that you will not break any one of these laws is 7 billion-to-1. You live in a world where everyone breaks these laws every day, if not every moment. You're an underdog! But thanks to our God, the Bible says that Jesus Christ has overcome the world. If you are trusting Christ in this dog-eat-dog world, you can reverse the odds against you.

The odds that you will lose are 0-to-1 billion or more! You will be a winner! But you will have to trust in Jesus Christ to be in the winner's circle. They will receive the crown of life eternal. All losers will be banished to hell. In this world, you will always be an underdog. Make sure you are an underdog with Christ!

Closing Prayer:

Father, we know that if we walk with You, the world dismisses us as losers. Instill in us the spirit of the underdogs of this world that don't accept the negativism and discouragement of our culture and let us run this race of life with Christ and be victorious, a winner. Amen.

Truth Theme: The Bible says that God chose the weak things of this world to confound the wise. Be a Gideon, a Joseph, a Daniel, a Martin Luther, for Christ.

coach@chapelfield.org

CHAPEL TALK

9

What's Up with Christian Schools?

"I advise no one to place a child where the Scriptures do not reign paramount. Every institution in which men are not increasingly occupied with the word of God must become corrupt."

Martin Luther

WHAT'S UP WITH CHRISTIAN SCHOOLS?

Background: Sometimes I did chapels on questions my students asked in class. The question above was asked by a ninth-grade girl. She went on, "I've gone to Christian schools all my life. I'd like to try a public school for a change."
I read the question in *chapel*.

Kids, the public schools have a lot to offer, some very fine teachers, great facilities and a large number of students. However, if you are serious about your education, and I know you and most of your classmates are, you must understand that in public schools (also known as government schools because the state has control over them) the curriculum has been taken over by humanism. It is promoted in every course and program.

You might say, "So what?" Very simply, this type of education denies God, His work in creation, and His authority over mankind. The motto of humanism is, *homo mensura*, meaning man is the measure. A pure humanist uses his life for his own interests and decides for himself what is right or wrong and has no objective standards outside of his own self-interests.

In your course with me, you saw in Genesis 6 what happened when the whole world were humanists. "God saw the wickedness of man was great in the earth. And that every imagination of the thoughts of his heart was only evil continually" (Genesis 6:5). Can you imagine everybody in the world doing what was evil all the time? That is what humanists call secularism—a world without God.

Now, public school denies their teaching will have that result, but that is what their teaching will lead to. For example, I am good friends with the (now retired) Pine Bush police chief. He told me that he had to keep two officers on standby to go into the high school every day. Each day they would go in an average of four or five times to make arrests for fights, drugs, and extreme bullying. This is a good start toward Genesis 6.

Do you know that you will spend over 15,000 hours pursuing your education in school? That's ninety percent more time than you spend in church and seventy percent more time than you will spend under the influence of your family. I am sure you would be convinced of anything if you spent that much time hearing about it. Your education will have a major effect on how you think and behave in the future and how you raise your children. Your parents must love you very much to pay public school taxes and pay additional tuition to send you to a Christian school. They have eternal values in mind. I hope you will think long-term and continue in your Christian education, thereby honoring God.

Sign at Chapel Field Christian Schools

The Bible reminds us that if we "train up a child in the way he should go: and when he is old, he will not depart from it" (Proverbs 22:6). Kids, God will be there long after humanism passes away. You will want to be there too.

Closing Prayer:

Father, You have called us to think on these things, whatsoever is true, honest, just, pure, lovely, good, virtuous, and praiseworthy. Help us to pursue an education that's based on these values, thereby keeping us from evil doings. Amen

Truth Theme: A wise man once said, "What you take into your mind will be what comes out in your life." Make it truth.

coach@chapelfield.org

CHAPEL TALK
IO
Tolerance or Principle?

"Standing on the promises that cannot fail ...
by the living Word of God I shall prevail."

"Standing on the Promises of God,"
R. Kelso Carter

TOLERANCE OR PRINCIPLE?

Students, human beings just don't like rules or laws. We elect lawmakers and then don't keep the laws they make. I had an employee once tell me that he never wears a seatbelt. I asked him why. He said that he doesn't like the government telling him what to do. Another friend who rides a motorcycle said, "I never wear a helmet when I'm riding at night because cops can't see me." Both laws save thousands of lives a year. We just don't like rules that our parents set for us. We don't like rules our government sets for us, and we don't like the rules that God sets for us, even if these laws and rules are designed for our safety and our protection. That's human nature.

The psalmist wrote, "Blessed (good things will happen to those who) are the undefiled... who walk in the law of the Lord." The Golden Rule for our culture used to be, "Do unto others as you would have them do unto you." Now it's, "Force others to accept what I do and be quiet about it." That is becoming the Golden Rule for our society.

As principal of this school, I got a directive from the New York State Department of Education recently. It stated that I must add to our social studies curriculum that alternative lifestyles be taught to all our students taking these courses so they will understand and appreciate diversity in our culture. Now, it's one thing to understand evil, but it's quite another to have the state demand that we appreciate it. However, the Bible is our standard here at Chapel Field, and it commands a very different lifestyle than the gay marriage one. This brings me to my scripture for this morning. Turn to Romans 1:26-36:

For this cause God gave them up unto vile affections: for even their women did change the natural use into that which is against nature: And likewise also the men, leaving the natural use of the woman, burned in their lust one toward another; men with men working that which is unseemly, and receiving in themselves that recompence of their error which was meet. And even as they did not like to retain God in their knowledge, God gave them over to a reprobate mind, to do those things which are not convenient; Being filled with all unrighteousness, fornication, wickedness, covetousness, maliciousness; full of envy, murder, debate, deceit, malignity; whisperers, Backbiters, haters of God, despiteful, proud, boasters, inventors of evil things, disobedient to parents, Without understanding, covenant breakers, without natural affection, implacable, unmerciful: Who knowing the judgment of God, that they which commit such things are worthy of death, not only do the same, but have pleasure in them that do them.

Students, be on the right side of this issue. Give no tolerance here. It will take courage to oppose this disgraceful sin. But oppose homosexuality you must. Do it with sincerity and love, but if given the opportunity, explain to those considering it or those involved in it the consequences of this sin according to Romans 1. It may cost them eternity.

Frances Havergal wrote in his great rally hymn, "Who is on the Lord's side? Who will serve the King? We are on the Lord's side. Savior, we are Thine." Kids, it comes down to whose side will you be on? When all our culture goes against you, I trust you will stand for principle over tolerance. Tolerance on some issues may be okay, but we will all have to answer to God for being neutral on the issue of killing babies and homosexual marriage.

Closing Prayer:

Forgive us, oh Lord. As a nation, we have slaugh-tered the innocent and disgraced the sanctity of marriage. Help us to stand against these two great evils in our culture. Lord, deliver us from evil. Amen.

Truth Theme: Don't ever give up on the altar of tolerance what you gained on the anvil of character.

coach@chapelfield.org

CHAPEL TALK
II
Follow Me Through

"Be ye followers of me,
even as I also am of Christ."

1 Corinthians 11:1

A Thought for Today:

FOLLOW ME THROUGH

All of us need mentors. I had many. Of course, my mother and father got me through my teenage years. Others were an admiral I worked for while in the Marine Corps, Bob Hoppe who led me to the Lord in '57, great teachers along the way and a fellow named Ellery Redfield ("Red"). I want to tell you how Ellery got me through a major milestone in my life.

I had just earned my commercial pilot's license. Next, I set my sights on my flight instructor's rating. This would mean I could fly every day and make considerably more income. Only three obstacles stood in my way. I needed 200 flying hours as pilot in command to apply, I needed to pass a rigid written test, and finally, I would need to pass a comprehensive flight examination. I got my 200 hours okay. Then I studied fiercely to pass the two-hour written test. After that, I began to practice for my flight test. I got a list of all the flight maneuvers that were required for an FAA examiner to ask. Then I began to practice them. After some time, I felt good enough about almost every maneuver. However, there was one I just couldn't get, the dreaded loop. I practiced and practiced, but either I did not have enough speed and would fall out on top of the loop, or I would make a very unacceptable egg-shaped loop.

One day while I was in the pilot's lounge, Ellery Redfield came in. Now, I knew Ellery had been a World War II fighter pilot and then a flight instructor for the army after the war, so I told Ellery my predicament. He said, "Let's go up, and I'll see what you can do." So, we got into a Piper 18-90 Super Cub, N-#9947 Delta. It was tandem seating, with the student in the front, instructor in the back. We climbed up to about 3,500 feet, clearing the area. He told me to come to a heading of 030 on the compass. Then he said, "Show me your loop."

I did the same old messed-up loop that I usually did. He climbed back up to 3,500 feet at a heading of 030, then he said these words to me: "Follow me through." I placed my hand on the throttle, put my other hand on the stick and my feet lightly on the rudder pedals. He then dropped the nose of the Super Cub down, added full power, brought the stick full back and we did a perfect loop, regaining entry altitude and the compass right on our original heading of 030 degrees. A perfect loop! Then he talked me through two more attempts, which I did reasonably well. Later, I passed my flight exam and did a pretty good loop. Ellery was a great mentor and teacher. I wouldn't have received my rating without his help.

Kids, if you're serious about your faith, and I hope you are (that's why you are here at Chapel Field), take the advice of the apostle Paul when he says, "Be ye followers of me, even as I also am of Christ" (1 Corinthians 11:1). Paul can be the principal mentor for you to learn how to fly the maneuvers in your Christian life. Read his instructions, pay close attention, and follow him through. The rewards will be far greater than a flight instructor's rating. Eternal life!

Bill and Lynne Gross, with 9947D

Closing Prayer:

Oh God, forgive us for not seeking great Christian minds that have gone before us. Oh, how we need mentors to avoid pitfalls that diminish the quality of our service to You. Lead us to Ellery Redfields in life, with the knowledge and experience to help us pass Your final exam. Amen.

Truth Theme: We are required to do a perfect "loop" in life (obey God's moral law), we just can't do it right and will be tested on it. Christ did the perfect "loop" for us on the cross. Get an instructor who can guide you through the test of your Christian life.

coach@chapelfield.org

CHAPEL TALK
12

What's Wrong with My Clothes?

*"[P]resent your bodies a living sacrifice,
holy, acceptable unto God"*

Romans 12:1

WHAT'S WRONG WITH MY CLOTHES?

In the circus, elephants are adorned in colorful drapes to be presented fashionably to the crowd. In class, I have taught you much about the tabernacle in the wilderness. It was the place of worship for Israel in their long trek to the Promised Land. You have heard me tell you that the high priest would enter the Holy of Holies behind the veil each year on the Day of Atonement. This was to sprinkle the blood of the sacrificial lamb on the mercy seat of the Ark of the Covenant. This was done so God could cover the sins of the people before the real atonement of Christ came. Everything had to be perfect when he entered there. His dress, his clothing, everything he wore was spotless and woven from the finest quality linen. He wore a shorter tunic called an ephod, which was very colorful and ornate, embellished with 12 precious stones, each representing one of the twelve tribes of Israel. Underneath, he wore a longer blue tunic, adorned with skillfully-crafted miniature pomegranates and golden bells sewn into the hem. It was a mixture of dazzling colors—blue, gold, purple and scarlet. He also wore a turban of the finest linen with a band of solid gold, engraved with the Hebrew words, "Holy to YHWH".

High Priest,
dressed in finest garments,
before entering the presence of God

Why did all this have to be perfect, expensive, colorful and adorn the high priest? Why did everything about him have to be the best? Because God was present there; they took the presence of God very seriously. God, the most holy, righteous, redeeming, merciful and loving God, was present. They wanted to present themselves respectfully.

Most of our churches today replicate, in some way, the ancient tabernacle or the temple. In Catholic and Lutheran churches, there is an altar and a low barrier separating the congregation from the priests and their religious activities. In other Protestant churches (except those designed for Christian entertainment) there is a raised platform and a table used for the sacraments. But why is this so different from the Old Testament tabernacle? Well kids, in Christ's atonement, the veil that separated God from His people was rent in two—gone. Christ has paid the debt we owed God by His death on the cross. Now there is no need for a veil or barrier. Now we all are welcomed into the presence of a holy God, not just the high priest but all the congregation.

I had the opportunity to visit a large evangelical church last Sunday. In front of me sat a man in a t-shirt and jeans with holes in them. I counted five others in t-shirts and in work-type pants. I spotted one man wearing camouflaged clothing. I saw some teen girls in miniskirts. I thought, "Is that how we now enter the Holy of Holies?" Is this how we present ourselves to a holy God who sacrificed His life and shed His own blood for us? Have we no pride in our appearance for His sake? We dress up for weddings and funerals but come in barn clothes and jeans to worship the Lord of Lords, the King of Kings! I thought, "What a disgrace!"

I once questioned a man in jeans and a t-shirt at another church one Sunday. He said, "Jesus accepts me just like I am." My reply to this man was, "You wouldn't go to a formal meeting with the President of the United States dressed like this, would you? Did your mother ever teach you about proper respect to honor those in authority?" He did not answer me. Later I thought, kids, you may not have money or the finest wardrobe but wear the best and cleanest thing you have to enter the presence of the holy God. Then save your money and buy the finest clothing you can get to enter the throne room of the King of the universe.

Closing Prayer:

Oh, most holy God, forgive us from taking Your presence and redemption so casually. Instill in our hearts the awe and awesomeness of Your character, the unspeakable grace of Your redemption that You brought through our Savior, the Lord Jesus Christ. Amen.

Truth Theme: When you are in the presence of your Savior and King, formally in church, spare no expense; dress your best. Your respectfulness and character will be your gift to God.

coach@chapelfield.org

CHAPEL TALK
13

What's the Most Important Word in the Bible?

"One little word shall fell him"

"A Mighty Fortress is Our God,"
Martin Luther

WHAT'S THE MOST IMPORTANT
WORD IN THE BIBLE?

<u>Background</u>: Sometimes I had very little time to do a chapel. This day, because it was a snowy day, the buses were late, and my principal asked me to forego chapel for this morning. I said that I would keep it short, but the kids needed a thought for the day. After the Pledge of Allegiance to our flag, every day the students repeat our school motto, Coram Deo (meaning, in the face of God): "I pledge to live my life always in His presence, under His authority and for His glory, Coram Deo." We have a short prayer and sometimes sing a hymn or meaningful praise song. This morning, because I didn't have much time, I asked the students a question:

Kids, what is the most important word in the Bible? Hands shot up everywhere. Some said salvation; others said redemption, born again, or forgiveness. One student in my theology class who was a good biblical thinker answered, the incarnation. I told them that I would give a hint. "Without this word, all the words you have given me so far would mean absolutely nothing to you." Again a few hands shot up. One said God; another said Christ. "Those words were very important," I said, "essential for our existence and salvation but not as important as the word I am thinking about."

I said, "I'll give you another clue. What if I told you this word has only two letters?" No hands went up. Only blank faces stared back at me. I said, "This little word makes all the words you told me of absolutely no use to you. The most important word in the

Bible is..." (pause) "IF. I-F. All the words you mentioned hang on the meaning of this little two-letter word (for you anyway)." The apostle John said:

If you confess your sins, He is faithful and just to forgive you of your sins and cleanse you from all unrighteousness (1 John 1:9).

That is, no confession, **no** forgiveness. The apostle Paul added:

*If you confess with your mouth Jesus is Lord and believe in your heart that God raised Him from the dead, thou shalt be saved" (**Romans** 10:9-10).*

That means, no confession and belief, **no** salvation. This little two-letter word is the most important word in the Bible. All the other great words are meaningless to you **IF** you don't heed this word.

Kids, the Bible uses many of these exclusionary words: "You **must** be born again," "**except** you repent, there is no salvation," "**IF** you keep my statutes... blessings. **IF** you don't, curses." That is why the most important word in the Bible has only two letters.

Closing Prayer:

Father, help us to not overlook this little word You used hundreds and hundreds of times in Your Word. We know You planned from all eternity to provide us with redemption and salvation through Jesus Christ, this to avoid perishing in hell. Cause us to believe, confess, repent, and enjoy you for all eternity. Amen.

Truth Theme: Every child knows that **IF** you obey your parent, an ice cream cone will appear and later, the car keys. **IF** you please your boss, a raise will appear. God uses the same principle, only the stakes are much higher.

coach@chapelfield.org

CHAPEL TALK
14
My Parents Are Too Strict!

"[F]or wide is the gate, and broad is the way, that leadeth to destruction... strait is the gate, and narrow is the way, which leadeth unto life, and few there be that find it."

Matthew 7:13-14

A Thought for Today

MY PARENTS ARE TOO STRICT

<u>Background</u>: Sometimes in *school,* we would get complaints like this, a normal teen comment, so I did several chapels on this subject. Students arguments went like this:

"There will be plenty of time for me to stay home later. I want more freedom now!" Kids, let me tell you a short story.

Learning to fly at Ramapo Valley Airport was difficult. I thought carrier pilots had it tough until I instructed at Ramapo. The runway was twelve feet wide and 1500' long. Trees eighty feet high lined both sides, and it seemed there was always a thirty-degree crosswind complicating the approach. You had to make a full-stall landing on the numbers every time. To accomplish this, students had to control their airspeed at ten mph above stall speed perfectly. No deviation! They had to maintain perfect directional control and descent from one mile out that would put the center line on the runway under their seat at touchdown. No deviation!

They would sweat bullets, but "kids" from 14 to 64 learned to do it. I had several students though, who were struggling with the precision demand, beg me, "Bill, please let's go to Orange County Airport where we have 5000' runways that are 150' wide with no trees. We could do it there!" "No way," I said. "You do it here or not at all."

One Saturday morning while waiting to take off with such a student, we watched a Cherokee 180 approaching for landing. He was going too fast. Hopping and skipping down the runway, at the last second, he decided to go around. On his second try, I could see he was too fast again. Several of us jumped out and waved at him to go away. As he went by, we saw he had a lady passenger, and he was intent on landing here. His third approach was no better, but this time he was determined to put it down. Sliding and skidding, he shot off the end of the runway, into some trees. The right wing was ripped off. The plane rolled over on the door, caught fire, and burned. Though many fought the flames, both occupants were burned alive. My student pilot had a tragic but powerful lesson in controlled flying. I told him, "That's why we don't practice on 5000' runways."

Your parents are instructing you to fly the straight and narrow so you can pilot your life without a crash. Crashed lives are all around you. Control your speed and your direction. Sweat bullets. No deviation! Remember more is at stake than immediate pleasure. A crash will burn you alive. Jesus reminds us, "wide is the gate, and broad is the way that leads to destruction, and many go that way, but straight is the gate and narrow the way that leads to life and few there are that find it." Put it on the numbers.

Parent scolding child

Closing Prayer:

Oh, heavenly Father, our human nature wants to make us free from all rules and laws. But Your psalmist says, "Blessed are they that walk in the laws of the Lord." Father, we want Your blessings to protect us in our lives, and we know that our parents want that too. We know that they are designed to prevent us from crashing our lives. Amen.

Truth Theme: Rules are tough to obey, but they will lead you, surprisingly, very quickly to life and abundant life. Your patience now will help avoid a crash later.

coach@chapelfield.org

CHAPEL TALK
15

Born Again? Most are Phonies!

"Regeneration (being born again) precedes
faith; faith produces true righteousness."

R.C. Sproul

BORN AGAIN? MOST ARE PHONIES!

Background: The question was raised, "What's so important about wanting to be born again when most who claim it are hypocrites?" I repeated the question, then said,

This question has a wrong assumption. No one _wants_ to be born again. The Bible tells us that no one seeks after God. No natural man _wants_ to find God. The term, "born again" is one of the most misunderstood slogans thrown about in our culture. Certain groups claim to have achieved it, others offer detailed directions or steps and insist others obtain it and there are still others who claim to have it, yet live like the worst of those who do not have it. Nonetheless, we all seem to be left with the impression that there is something we must do to get it. That's not true. According to the Bible, being born again, or quickened as Jesus and Paul further explained, is not something we do but is something that God does for us. In John 1:13, Jesus says, "[Those] which were born [again] were not born of blood nor of the will of the flesh, nor of the will of man but of God."

The terms _born again_ or _quickened_ in the Bible describe an event, often known but sometimes unknown, when the Spirit of God sparks an individual with the desire to love God and surrender his life in service to Him. The outcome of this event is great conviction for the offenses we have committed toward God, confession, and a willingness to stop offending God and receiving the gift of faith, belief, and trust in Christ for one's right standing before God. Further, the Bible says a life of humility, modesty, obedience, personal sacrifice, and dedicated service to

God will follow this event. If it does not follow at some point, those who claim it never had it.

We are not interested in slogans or detailed steps, nor should we be discouraged and deterred by phonies who, having never had it, totally distort it. The new birth is the greatest event humanity can experience. Desire it. Pray for it. And if you have it, cling to it.

Closing Prayer:

Heavenly Father, forgive us if others see us as phonies or hypocrites claiming to be Christians. Being made alive by Your Holy Spirit was not based on our effort, but by Your gracious mercy and power. We know that we have the responsibility to reflect Your character and majesty properly. Please strengthen us and give us the courage to do so. Amen.

Truth Theme: When you are born again the Holy Spirit gives you a desire that you truly never had before. It will cause you to love going to church, love worshiping God, love hearing His word preached, love singing praises to Him and love your fellow human beings. Should you not quickly develop a love for all these things, you have not been truly born again. Remember, regeneration produces righteousness—no righteousness, no regeneration.

coach@chapelfield.org

CHAPEL TALK

16

The Sovereignty and Providence of God

*"God the all wise! By the fire of
Thy chastening, Earth shall to freedom
and truth be restored."*

"God, the Omnipotent," Henry Chorley

A Thought for Today

THE SOVEREIGNTY AND PROVIDENCE OF GOD

Background: I took an extended chapel this day to discuss a very important subject. This was to help our students with the foundation to their Christian world- and life-view, and to review this subject with our seniors who were preparing for their *comprehensive biblical* exams coming up. I have included a diagram to help the reader with this topic.

The **sovereignty of God** simply means, that God created all things in the universe and that He controls and ordains all that comes to pass in His creation. In other words, nothing that happens happens without God's authority, design, or purpose. The psalmist writes in Psalm 89:11, "The heavens are Thine, the earth is also Thine: as for the world and the fullness thereof, Thou has founded them." The apostle Paul also writes, "To Him (Jesus Christ) who worketh all things after the counsel of His own will," (Ephesians 1:11b). Note: the apostle says that He "worketh all things" (are under His direction). The attributes (characteristics) of God tell us that God is:

- Eternal–Psalm 102:27
- Self-existent–Exodus 3:14
- Immutable (unchangeable)–Hebrews 13:8
- Omnipotent (all-powerful)–Nehemiah 9:32
- Omniscient (all-knowing)–Psalm 139:2
- Omnipresent–Jeremiah 23:23

So, the scripture tells us explicitly that God is able, has the power, and has supreme authority and control over everything He created.

The **providence of God,** on the other hand, does not speak to how God is sovereign over His created order but rather **how** God governs what He created, and how He cares for and provides for all living creatures—you and me! God's providence is seen in two ways. One, He provides for us by giving us **natural law**. And secondly, He provides for His people (the covenant of faith people) by **divine law**.

First, let us consider natural law. Natural law doesn't necessarily need God's direction all the time because these laws work automatically but are still under His total control. These are laws like the laws of physics, logic, mathematics, biology, science, moral laws, etc. For example, if you want to fly, you don't just jump off a building and flap your arms. You learn the laws of aerodynamics, and then you can fly at 40,000 feet, eating dinner and enjoying a movie. These benefits given to all mankind are called *common grace* (gifts to all men). "For the sun shines on the just and on the unjust alike."

Further, students, because of His creation and through His creation, God has revealed Himself clearly to all mankind. This is called general revelation—all men can see God clearly in nature. The apostle Paul wrote:

> *"Because that which may be known of God is manifest to them, for God has shown it unto them. For the invisible things of Him from the creation of the world are clearly seen being understood by those things that are made. Even His eternal power and Godhead, so that they are without excuse" (Romans 1:19-20).*

The psalmist put it this way, "The heavens declare the glory of God" (Psalm 19:1). (Now, students, remembering these texts to support your answers on your exam.)

But kids, there is also **divine law**. Divine law is when God intervenes in natural law to provide benefits for His own people. These are called *special grace* (gifts only for a few as opposed to *common grace*, gifts to all men). God in Jesus Christ acts against natural laws (through miracles) to protect and provide for His people.

Sometimes God does this intervention **directly**, quickly, or immediately as the water of the Red Sea did, standing on edge to allow His people to escape from Pharaoh. He sent manna from heaven, the dead were raised, the blind were given their sight, the lame walked. These are direct and immediate interventions of God. At other times, God uses divine law to intervene in natural law by indirect means. These miracles occur over a longer period of time, like God's manipulation of history in Joseph's life. It took over thirty years of events for Joseph to actually save his people. Or as in God's planning the coming of Christ. This intervention took over 4,000 years of His careful planning. As the apostle Paul stated, "In the fullness of time God has sent forth His Son."

We have learned that God created all this vast universe and world. He created men and women. And they know Him clearly from creation and are not thankful to Him. However, in spite of this, He in His providence cares for them. He gave them natural laws and divine law.

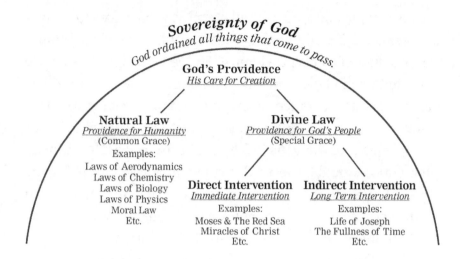

Graphic design: Andy Spanjer

Kids, when God said to Adam, "By the sweat of your brow ye shall eat bread" (Genesis 3:19), these benefits were instituted for all men. You can see how these laws have benefited men, especially in modern times. Just reach in your back pocket. There you have a cell phone. We have computers and all the great technological advances. From the invention of the wheel to the boom of technology in the 19th and 20th centuries, man has conquered natural laws to his great benefit. But kids, among those natural laws was a moral law (the Ten Commandments). These, too, would be a great benefit to mankind that, if obeyed, would guarantee peace, safety, and prosperity for him. In fact, man loved the benefits of natural law (except His moral one) but never acknowledged God or the fact that He gave them to him!

Now, man's response to God's moral law was to say "Stick it, God. We want abortion, adultery, homosexuality, gay marriage, hate, greed, lust, lies, coveting, etc." In light of this rebellion (sin), God, being holy and righteous, determined man would lose eternal life and suffer for all eternity. What a loss for stupid law-breakers! God did not leave man in this state of condemnation. Because of God's providence (His care and love for us), He instituted divine law. Now God would intervene in natural law and its devastating outcome by giving man special grace. This came in the form of miraculous protection and provision for those people who would have faith in His promises. The ultimate intervention would be Jesus Christ paying for and forgiving the sins of all who would believe, repent, and trust in Him. God did all this because of His sovereignty and through His providence. Why? Because "God so loved the world" (John 3:16).

Kids, adjust your world- and life-view. True reality is God at work in history to provide you and me a new heaven and earth where we will have peace, joy, and health forever. The hymn goes, "Hallelujah, what a Savior is Jesus, my Lord." Make sure you have repented of sin, believed, and trusted in Him alone. Study God's Word. Rejoice in His sovereignty, providence, moral laws, and His divine law, that you will believe and obey Him and live forever!

Closing Prayer:

Oh God, Your love for all us wayward humans is so great, but for those You called, its depths and heights we can't comprehend. Your love that sent Jesus Christ to the cross for us, to forgive us and redeem us is the greatest story ever told. Forgive us for having such a limited view of who You are and Your care for us. Give us the vision to gaze upon the totality of the gospel and make it part of us, to cause us to serve you every day of our lives. Amen.

Truth Theme: God in His sovereignty gave you natural law so you would know and acknowledge Him; He gave you divine law so that you would know Christ. These great gifts were designed to call you to eternal life and avoid hell. What will you do with them?

coach@chapelfield.org

CHAPEL TALK

17

Do You Have Blinders On?

*"[T]urn not from it to the right hand
or to the left, that thou mayest prosper
withersoever thou goest."*

Joshua 1:7

DO YOU HAVE YOUR BLINDERS ON?

Whining is what most of us do when we have to go to the doctor's office. But we know that the optometrist wouldn't hurt us, so we relax when we have to go for a checkup. Often, the doctor has a little arm with a ball on it that he moves from one side of your face to the other. When the little ball is beside your ear, he will move it toward your eye. Staring straight ahead, he will ask you when you are aware of the ball or can see it in your peripheral vision. This vision is very important because it keeps you aware of your surroundings and aware of any possible approaching danger. This possible danger is what I want to talk about to you this morning.

When I was in the agricultural consulting business a few years ago, I had a client who had racing horses. He had trotters. They are different from *flats* (horses that have jockeys riding on them). Trotters and pacers pull a *sulky* (large-wheeled, very light carts) behind them.

Trotting horse pulling sulky

This is a very popular form of racing in America. We have major breeding farms in our country. Only a mile from our school is Blue Chip Farms, 2000 acres of land and hundreds of horses dedicated to this racing sport. Often, I would have to go to racing events for my client. I noticed there that most horses, when racing, had small, black leather squares on the side of their eyes. When I asked a stable hand why they were there, he said that they are called blinders and they were used to block the horse's peripheral vision. I asked, "Why do you want to do that?" He continued, "So that when the horse is racing, he is not distracted when he is trying to focus on the finish line."

Horse with blinders

I thought, wow! Blinders are what I need, and I think most Christians need to avoid all the distractions in our culture. These distractions prevent us from focusing on the mission Christ has given us. These distractions—money, sex, clothes, cars, culture, work, entertainment, etc.—keep us from concentrating on the finish line: our calling in Jesus Christ.

No matter how dedicated we are to the gospel mission, our peripheral vision keeps picking up on these distractions. Oh Lord, give us blinders, so these distractions don't keep us from finishing the race. Four times God told Joshua, "Be strong and of good courage" when he was called to conquer the land promised to Israel. In Joshua 1:7, God added, "Turn not from it (the laws of God) to the right hand or to the left, that thou mayest prosper whithersoever thou goest."

What a message for us today. The world with its distractions wants to destroy us. The world says, "Turn to the left"—there's pleasures there, lust, sex, parties, alcohol, and that's what's popular. "Turn to the right"—there's money there, popularity, wealth, and possible fame. But the Bible says, "Broad is the way that leads to destruction and narrow is the way that leads to life."

Kids, keep your eyes fixed on Jesus. God told Joshua, "Be strong and of good courage, turn not from it (the laws of God— your blinders) to the right or to the left, that thou mayest have good success whithersoever thou goest." Boys and girls, keep your eyes fixed on Jesus if you want the trophy of eternal life.

Closing Prayer:

Oh God, to what use is it if we gain the whole world and lose our own souls? Give us blinders so that we can't see the distractions of our culture that are designed to lead us down the broad way. Oh Lord, deliver us from evil. Amen.

Truth Theme: Any athlete or general will tell you, if you really want the victory, stay focused on the goal. If you want to please God, keep your blinders on to the culture!

coach@chapelfield.org

CHAPEL TALK
18

I Can't Take It Anymore!

*"Onward Christian soldiers...
We have Christ's own promise,
Which can never fail."*

*Onward Christian Soldiers,
Sabine Baring-Gould*

A Thought for Today

I CAN'T TAKE IT ANYMORE!

<u>Background</u>: I did some chapels on issues raised
by my students in *class*. Here is one:

Student: "Teachers demand, coaches yell. The pressures are
too great. I can't take it anymore."

*I did a two-part chapel talk on this biblical story a few
years ago, but this episode so impressed me that I wanted to
give these kids a challenge on it.*

At the end of each year at Chapel Field, we have a sports ban-
quet. Coaches hand out Varsity and J.V. letters, MVP awards,
etc. At the end of the ceremony, I have the opportunity to hand
out the Coaches' Award to a few kids. It doesn't necessarily go to
the best athlete, the best shooter, or the best hitter. It goes to the
athlete who can endure—the boy or girl who pushes themselves
hard, who can persist and never give up, one who has self-dis-
cipline, who practices relentlessly and cheerfully. I look for the
athlete who can withstand insults, play injured, get yelled at and
rise higher, who can take bad calls and work harder; the athlete
who can win with humility and lose with dignity. This athlete
gets the Coaches' Award.

It was a hero of mine who inspired me to give this award, a
person who combined humility with toughness, persistence with
patience, and fear with faithfulness. Contradictory attributes?
No. A superhero? Yes! This person was a lady and a mother.
You can read about her in Matthew 15. She had little prestige.

She came from an apartheid community. She had a deathly ill daughter at home. She was an unlikely hero. Yet she knew where victory lay. It was with Jesus. She followed Him day and night. She called to Him wherever He was. She was told to go away, yet she persisted. She was yelled at, yet she kept calling. "Send her away," the disciples pleaded. We can't stand her continual annoyance. Finally, she rushes toward Jesus and pleads, "Lord, help me." A Phoenician Canaanite woman, a Gentile from a heathen nation. What was her effort worth? The answer from the Lord of Lords (the "Coach of coaches"), "What do I have to do with dogs (the heathen, the ungodly)?" Ouch! The ultimate insult. He called her a dog! What to do? Run? Hide? Pout? Sulk? Tell Him off? Yell back? Not this woman, a lady with persistence, patience, and tough humility. Her answer? "Yea Lord (I am a dog), but even dogs get the scraps from the master's table." Yes, I am a sinner. Yes, the pressure is great, but I humbly press on for even the scraps of Your holiness and righteousness. She played injured. What was the Lord's response? "Oh, woman, great is thy faith. Your daughter is healed." Victory!

Oh Christian, do you want the trophy of eternal life, a crown of stars? Endure the pressure. When I get to heaven (God willing), I will search for this little woman who because of her tough humility, persistent patience, and fearless faithfulness long ago won an award far greater than earthly trophies. Persist in the academic and athletic arenas. Take insults and bad calls. Work harder. Keep this lady in mind. The victory is worth it.

Closing Prayer:

Oh Lord, forgive us for our pride and failure to accept criticism. Teach us the spirit of this little

Phoenician woman; burn it deep on our hearts that we may be humble, patient, and persistent in seeking You, for we know You have the keys to the locker room of heaven—an eternal life. Amen.

Truth Theme: Strive for the heavenly Coaches' Award. It will bring you the crown of life!

coach@chapelfield.org

CHAPEL TALK

19

"I Left My Wallet at Home!"

"For nothing good have I, whereby Thy grace to claim... Jesus paid it all; all to Him I owe."

Jesus Paid It All, Elvina M. Hall

"I LEFT MY WALLET AT HOME!"

Background: This chapel was on an important
theological subject that would help our students on
an upcoming final exam.

I once heard a pastor say at a church service, "If you really
want to know the meaning of the word 'atonement,' just break
it down: at-one-moment—Christ died for us at-one-moment." I
thought that was an irreverent and childish thing to say about
what is arguably one of the most important words in the Bible.
Everyone dies "at one moment," but Christ's atonement meant
much more than that.

Kids, the word *atonement* actually means *to cover*. When the
high priest went into the Holy of Holies each year to get God's
forgiveness for the sins of the people, he sprinkled the blood of
the sacrificial lamb on the mercy seat on the top of the Ark of the
Covenant, thereby symbolizing that the sacrificial blood hides
the sins of God's people from His eyes. In Jesus Christ's case,
the atonement wasn't to hide our sin but to pay for our sin.

I want to explain this to you today by using two illustrations.
Often our family of seven drove to Florida to see my father.
We would go down Route 81, the Pennsylvania Turnpike, from
our home in New York. There were many hills and valleys on
that route. When going over one such hill, we saw many flash-
ing lights and ambulances ahead. As we approached, we could
see that a family trailer being pulled by a truck had come loose
while driving at high speed and had rolled over many times. The
trailer was shattered. Only scraps remained. There were four or

five children in the trailer at the time. They had all died. White sheets were placed over them to hide their broken, mangled, ugly, deformed bodies. This is exactly what the high priest did to hide our sins from God's eyes.

A second illustration I want to give you depicts Christ's atonement. I said to my class last year (note: I only had fourteen students in those early years), "I am going to quit teaching! I've had it. However, you have been a great class, and I want to take you out for dinner. You pick the place." Brian raised his hand. "I want to go to Sardi's in New York City. My father works there, and he will get us a discount." I knew that Sardi's dinners were about $100 a plate but this was a good class, so we went. We loaded into a van and were off to the Big Apple. The meal was great, a variety of hors d'oeuvres, a large variety of lobsters and filet mignon, delicious desserts. Then came the check. I reached for my money. I left my wallet at home! What could I do now? I began to sweat. Looking all around, I thought to myself, "This is embarrassing." Brian's dad picked up on my despair. He said, "Don't worry, Coach. I'll cover it." Now, did Brian's dad mean that he would take his napkin and cover that grotesque check to hide it from view? No, he meant that he would *cover* that check by paying for it.

Students enjoying a dinner, out on the town

That's the difference between the Old Testament atonement and Christ's atonement. The high priest just covered the people's sins, hiding them from God's view by the blood of a lamb. Christ's atonement, by His shed blood, paid for our sin. The apostle Paul writes, "Ye are bought with a price. Therefore, glorify God in your body, and in your spirit which are God's."

Kids, you are bought and paid for. Why is this such an important study at our school? Because our sin had created an enormous debt that we owe to God; so great a debt that you will have to pay for it with your death and an eternity without peace. Thank God Christ paid your debt if you choose to trust Him. Your debt, then, is stamped "paid in full."

Closing Prayer:

Oh God, the great hymn goes, "Jesus paid it all; all to Him I owe." Jesus paid it all. Forgive us, Father, for not taking Your great sacrificial payment seriously and not yielding fully in commitment to You. Amen.

Truth Theme: Your debt to God, which was created by your sin and rebellion to His laws, is stamped **PAID** by the atonement of Jesus Christ **IF** you have believed and repented of your sin. That's the good news of the Gospel, the greatest gift anyone can ever receive.

coach@chapelfield.org

CHAPEL TALK
20

"Hey, Coach! What's the Double Imputation Anyway?"

"For he hath made him to be sin for us, who knew no sin; that we might be made the righteousness of God in Him."

2 Corinthians 5:21

"HEY, COACH! WHAT'S THE DOUBLE IMPUTATION ANYWAY?"

Students, in the chapel time we have this morning, I want to make sure you have this critically important truth in your Christian world- and life-view. You need to know it, memorize it, think about it, trust in it, digest it, make it part of you, like breathing. What is this critical ultimate truth of the gospel? You might say, "I know the gospel. Christ died for our sins." You are partially right. But your definition is not complete. Your answer does not get to the heart of the gospel. In the next few minutes, I want to explain the heart of the gospel. Whether you are saved and struggling to live the Christian life, or you are unsaved, this subject and definition can change your life. Kids, the scriptural premise is that no unrighteous person can see or be in the presence of God. Isaiah wrote, "Your sins have hidden His face from you" (Isaiah 59:2). The apostle Paul said, "Unrighteousness shall not inherit the kingdom of God" (1 Corinthians 6:9). This is why God placed Moses in the cleft of the rock, only showing him His hind parts. Even then that made Moses's face glow like the sun. Moses stated, "No man can see God's face and live" (Exodus 33:20).

All the major religions say that an unrighteous man can enter the kingdom of God. Buddhist and liberal "Christians" say **good works** will enable man to present themselves good enough (righteous) to face God and enter the kingdom. Islam and legalistic Judaism say **obedience** to scriptural demands will get you to see God's face. Roman Catholicism says "Unrighteousness, no problem. Through our sacramental system, we will **make**

man righteous. This is by absolution of his sins." And further, they say if that doesn't get him totally righteous, he can spend some time in purgatory to earn what is needed to make up his righteousness.

Now kids, all these views are very appealing to a natural man. But what does the Bible say? We all acknowledge that we must end up righteous in order to meet God. But how is this done? How can we attain righteousness? The answer is the gospel. The further question is how does the gospel help us attain the status of righteousness? What is the heart of the gospel that teaches us ultimate truth?

Reformation theologians tell us, the heart of the gospel is seen in the term *double imputation*. What's that? If you have your Bibles, please turn to our scripture for today—2 Corinthians 5:21. This verse tells us what theologians mean by double imputation and explains the heart of the gospel:

> *"For He hath made Him to be sin for us who knew no sin, that we might be made the righteousness of God in Him."*

The heart of the gospel is this: our unrighteousness was imputed (applied to or put on) Christ, and His righteousness was imputed (applied to) our account. Those two little words in that text, "for us" in Greek is *huper*. Kids, this is the heart of the gospel, the main point: that Jesus Christ did this all **for us.** Every one of you should make little signs—*huper*—and put them in your room, lockers, and on your books to remind you every minute of the day of what Christ did **for you** on that horrific cross at Calvary.

Satan, the prince of darkness, the wise serpent, the eternal liar, does not want you to believe this gospel. He will do everything in his power to sidetrack you—friends, the opposite sex, video games, sports, college teachers, even other "Christians"—anything to keep you from trusting in the Christ of the double imputation. He will even use the routines of your church programs and youth groups to distract you from this doctrine. He will say, "Just do what you are doing, flow in the stream of your activities. No need to get that serious about your theology. After all, you're a Christian, aren't you?" Kids, if you take the heart of the gospel, make it part of your heart, and serve Christ every day you are living, you will cast daggers into the heart of Satan. You will destroy his attempts to steal your life from God.

If you have repented, believed, and trusted in Christ alone, He has taken your unrighteousness to the cross and given you His righteousness, and you will behold, unobstructed, the face of God and have eternal life!

Closing Prayer:

Oh God, who can measure the depth of what You have done for us in Christ Jesus? Knowing we would be sinners by nature, You planned from all eternity to have Christ take all our unrighteousness on the cross and give us all His righteousness. This so we might enter Your presence and live with You for eternity. Give us the faith amidst all of Satan's lies that are aimed to distract us from this truth, to humbly and gratefully pursue You every day of our lives. Amen.

Truth Theme: Make this theology part of your world- and life-view.

coach@chapelfield.org

CHAPEL TALK
21
What Are You Focused On?

> "Well, I woke this mo'nin,
> with my mind stayin' on Jesus...
> Well, I am walkin' and talkin'
> with mind stayin' on Jesus."
>
> Woke Up This Morning, Roosevelt Graves

A Thought for Today

WHAT ARE YOU FOCUSED ON?

Well kids, I guess by now you know I like to tell aviation stories. That is because there are so many things about flying that relate to everyday life. So here goes another one.

While as a flight instructor, I had a student named Al Botwin. He had mastered all his air work—flying straight and level, turns to headings, slow flight, climbs and glides, etc. Then we started to do approach to landings and actual landings. That he couldn't get. We spent hour upon hour practicing, and he just couldn't make a decent landing. Now let me tell you what that involves. An airplane is heavier than air. Some light airplanes (trainers) weigh as little as 1,000 pounds. Large passenger planes, like the Airbus A380, weigh up to 562 tons (1,234,600 pounds).

To support them in flight, enough wind has to go over their wings to create enough lift to overcome their weight, i.e., gravity, giving them lift. When there is not enough air going over the wing to support the weight of the plane, it stalls. It just drops like a rock. So, the objective of any pilot is to have your wheels six inches or less above the runway when that stall occurs. The tires just squeak, and then the full weight of the plane is on the runway. Then you can use the brakes to slow yourself down.

These landings are very hard to gauge for some students. But it can be mastered if you stay focused on the right thing—your airspeed and the height of the runway under your wheels. Mr. Botwin just couldn't get it. Most students learn this (not master it) in three or four hours of practice. Time after time he would stall out about three or four feet above the runway. I would have to give a little power to regain flying speed, then land the plane myself. I was completely frustrated. So, on one landing, I took a big gamble. I took my hands off the controls and my eyes off the runway. I got around him and looked straight in his eyes. I could see that he was not looking at the runway. So, when we stopped (after a near crash landing), I asked, "Al, what are you focusing on? I can see that it's not on the runway." What he said shocked me. He said, "I am looking at the screws on the front cowling." I said, "Al, that doesn't give you the distance between the runway and the plane!" So, we tried it again and this time I made him focus on where the runway meets the apron. If I had let him solo with his eyes focused on the cowling screws, he would have crashed. But he got it when he focused on the right thing.

Plane cowling

What do coaches always yell at their players during a game? "Stay focused!" They know that their players cannot be successful if their minds are focused on the wrong things. This is true in all of life. You have to stay focused on your studies, your athletic performance, your relationships, your families and on Jesus Christ if you want ultimate success. If you do not want to be successful, let your mind wander to the wrong things. Focusing on the screws on the cowling (things like popularity, self-image, entertainment, music, video games, sex, parties, and other things in pop culture) will not give you the right distance between reality and the truth.

Isaiah the prophet (one of your flight instructors) said, "Thou wilt keep him in perfect peace whose mind is stayed (focused) on Thee because he trusteth in Thee" (Isaiah 26:3). Focusing on trusting in God, who is Jesus Christ, will guarantee you success in life whatever you do.

Closing Prayer:

Oh God, forgive us for not focusing on the right things. We want to make a good landing in life. Help us land our lives on the narrow way, full stall, right on Your promises. There we know we will find perfect peace and success. Amen.

Truth Theme: Our minds (and eyes) are prone to wander. Stay fixed on Jesus, and you won't make a crash landing.

coach@chapelfield.org

CHAPEL TALK
22

Are You Giving Up?

"If you are not learning and practicing, you are dead or dying."

Based on Proverbs 16:22-23

A Thought for Today

ARE YOU GIVING UP?

<u>Background</u>: All my students know the differences between the graces God gives to his creatures. There is **common grace** He gives to all men to support life, i.e., sunshine, rain, companionship and all the things we get from the natural order. Then there's **special grace** God gives to those whom He calls to salvation through His Son Jesus Christ. And *lastly,* there is **provisional grace** that God provides to His people to help them in their Christian growth.

A student said to me one time, "I am giving up. I can't get anywhere in my Christian life." I knew this boy was quite serious about his Christian faith, so I did a chapel on this subject. Let me explain the problem this way. An experience in business taught me a lesson about spiritual growth. I have on my office wall a picture of a Douglas DC-6B. It is a four-engine cargo plane, the big brother of the DC-4, which flew supplies during the war. Students often ask me, "What's the name of that plane, Coach?" I say, *Provisional Gracie.* "What kind of name is that," they ask. Let me tell you the story.

This is one of fifteen I once had. They were great planes. They could carry 30,000 pounds of freight, roar up to 20,000 feet, slip along at 250 mph and deliver anywhere in the U.S. Ole *Gracie* was a profit maker. In fact, I began to take *Provisional Gracie* for granted. One day there was a major strike in the industry. We parked *Gracie* and her sisters on the ramp. "They don't cost us anything if they don't fly," I said. Wrong! Bad mistake. A few months later business started up again. Out came *Gracie.* But

she had gotten cold out there. Her radios had gotten moisture in them and shorted out. Oil laid in the bottom of her big R-2800 engines and fouled up everything. Wires dried up and cracked, cables got rusty and wouldn't work. Ouch! It cost $5,000 per plane to get them back flying. I learned a tough lesson. Keep them flying, they work fine; park them, they quit.

Kids, the church today is like that fleet of planes. Her members are parked on the side. Their voices are shorted out. Their engines won't run, throttles have gotten rusty. Complacency has set in. Christians are like *Gracie*, sitting on the ramp of life, enjoying the common grace of God but going nowhere. But we forget common grace is passing grace. Look in the mirror. Read the obituaries. We sit there enjoying special grace—"On Christ the solid rock I stand," sins forgiven, justified by faith, praise God! Amen!—but we are not flying. We are not utilizing God's **provisional grace**. This grace (benefits from God) comes from five sources. Using them, we fly. Without them, we die. The takeoff checklist includes: daily prayer, structured and devotional Bible study, devoted worship and the sacraments, serious fellowship with serious Christians, and sacrificial service in the mission. Regular practice of provisional grace makes common grace worth passing and validates our claim on special grace. If you have been parked on the side and your Christian life is dried up and cracking, don't take His provisional grace for granted. Check them off. It may cost you something to get back into the air, but God holds you accountable to "keep 'em flying!"

Closing Prayer:

Oh God, forgive us for often getting discouraged
when You did not get discouraged when going to

the cross for us. Challenge and inspire us to use the provisions You graciously give us. Revive us again. May our souls be rekindled with fire from above. May we use revival to get off our duffs and serve You with the energy and enthusiasm You deserve. Amen.

Truth Theme: Remember, God has given us all we need to run our Christian race successfully. Take advantage of it.

coach@chapelfield.org

CHAPEL TALK
23
Are You a Charismatic?

"For unto you it is given in the behalf of Christ, not only to believe on him, but also to suffer for his sake."

Philippians 1:29

ARE YOU A CHARISMATIC?

Background: Since Chapel Field is an interdenominational school, we have students from many different churches. Our emphasis in our biblical program is from Reformation theology and, at times, differing viewpoints are raised in class. The Charismatic issue came up in one such class. We had several Pentecostal students in school, and they, and others, wanted to know why Christians were divided on this, so I did a chapel on the subject.

Students, this morning I would like to speak to you about a sensitive issue in our Christian culture. Some issues like abortion, gay marriage or even liberalism in the church are issues that I am eager to attack. Issues regarding biblical truth that are in conflict among Christians, however, are more difficult and must be defended with sensitivity, using scriptural reference and in a loving manner. Having said that...

Kids, there has been some confusion in our school as to the Charismatic movement in our Christian culture. So, I want to speak to you about it this morning. The word 'charismatic' comes from the word *charisma*, meaning there are Christians seeking a joyous religious experience. In that sense, all Christians are charismatic as we all seek joy in our experience with Christ. We get overwhelming joy in Christ for having our sins forgiven, and the guarantee of eternal life! The problem is that most charismatics today have come out of the Pentecostal movement. There are three major doctrines of Pentecostalism. The first is the teaching of *the second work of grace*. That is, being born again is the first work of the Holy Spirit that brings salvation to the believer. But to complete your growth as a Christian, you need the baptism of the Holy Spirit. This act they call the second work of God's grace.

Secondly, they believe that this act of the Holy Spirit will always be accompanied by the person speaking an unknown language called tongues. Thirdly, they believe this second blessing gives the believer power and gifts of ministry, especially boldness, gifts of healing, of prophecy, leading to prosperity. Pentecostals call these beliefs the *full gospel*—baptism by the Holy Spirit, plus the addition of speaking in tongues, and gifts toward ministry, health, and prosperity.

I want to say the following about this movement. We know that all Christians are filled with the Holy Spirit. Paul, in Acts 6:3, 7:55, and 11:24, described Christians as being "full of the Holy Spirit." The Greek word here is "*pleres*" meaning, "full to the top" (W.E. Vine, *Dictionary of New Testament Words*, pg. 136). The Apostle goes on further to describe "every man" as given the manifestation of the Holy Spirit for ministry (Acts 12:7). All true Christians have the Holy Spirit in His fullness, to be used for their particular service in our Lord's vineyard.

My second comment is speaking in unknown languages can be very dangerous, even if an interpreter is present. When I was in college, it was required that all students attend a local church on Sunday evenings to support our church communities. One night I drove four or five of my buddies to a Pentecostal meeting. During the service, a group of elders began a tongues ceremony. People from the congregation came up, and the elders prayed over them to get them to speak in tongues, and they did. One of my classmates who had been raised up in a missionary family in the bush country of Africa grabbed my arm and said, "We've got to get out of here, quick!" He rushed to the door, and we all followed. On the way out I asked, "What is the matter?" He turned and said, "I know the dialect they are speaking. It is spoken by a tribe that my parents ministered to. These people were blaspheming and cursing Jesus's name in that language!" My word of caution to those who speak in tongues is that whenever you let yourself go into a trance, and speak words you yourself do not understand, you cannot know for certain who it is that is possessing you.

Thirdly, regarding the gifts of the Spirit, Romans 12 lays out very clearly the gifts of the Spirit, but good health, safety, and prosperity are not among them. Ask the thousands and thousands of Christians who were persecuted and martyred for their faith down through the ages. We are called to suffer for our Savior, even if it puts our health and prosperity in jeopardy. Run from this doctrine.

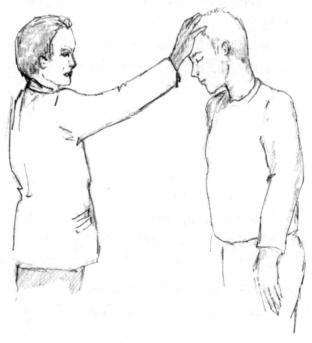

Charismatic healing

Kids, this charismatic movement has three major groups or types: (1) is the **"joy of your salvation"** group. They are totally biblical and orthodox. (2) is the **"second work of grace"** group. They are partially biblical and un-biblical because of their poor theology as mentioned earlier. (3) is the **positive thinking movement** of Norman Vincent Peale in the 60's and now Joel Osteen. They are un-biblical because they are man-centered and thus idolatrous human welfare is the prime importance not righteousness, holiness, Christ and His mission. (4) **The Word of Faith movement**. This group is totally un-biblical and heretical. They believe there is new revelation beside the Word of God in the Bible. They claim all Christians are "little gods" and if you are not healthy and prosperous, you don't have enough faith — it is your fault. The proponents are Benny Hinn, Joyce Meyer, Ken Copeland, Ken Hagin, and all the Crouches on TBN. They get tremendous wealth from "sowing faith seeds" on the backs of the poor and needy. Kids, defend yourselves from this great false teaching by trusting in your Bible alone. It is the final and only authority for your faith, *Sola Scriptura*.

Closing Prayer:

Dear God, please let our motivation in our Christian life be who You are, Your character and love for us in Jesus Christ. Let our excitement spring from Your divine attributes and cause us to serve You with all of our minds and hearts. Amen

Truth Theme: Be charismatic in the joy of your salvation, yet leery of those who want you to have additional experiences.

coach@chapelfield.org

CHAPEL TALK
24
Who is Majority Rule, Sr.?

"When the majority is happy with everyone making $20,000 a year and living on welfare, with no incentives for everyone to attain their dreams, you'll know Americaism is dead."

Victor Davis Hanson (paraphrase)

A Thought for Today

WHO IS MAJORITY RULE, SR.?

Background: *To* give some variety to my chapel talks,
I got one of my top theology students to do a question-and-
answer skit with me.

Kids, because of our limited time this morning, I am going
to be interviewed by the editor of our school's newsletter, Jen
McLeod:

Jen: Hey, Coach, you're always talking about Majority Rule.
Tell us about him.

Coach: Sure! Don't you remember Majority Rule, Sr.? I grew
up under his administration. He was a benevolent dictator.
With him, we could pray in school and even discuss creationism.
Under Majority Rule, Sr., the pervert stayed out of sight where
he belonged, and millions of babies made it to life. In fact, you
could go to movies with your kids, and the flag was honored!

Jen: What went wrong?

Coach: Just after World War II, Majority Rule, Sr. ran away
with his girlfriend.

Jen: What?! Who was she?

Coach: Her name was Public Opinion.

Jen: Where did she come from?

Coach: Public Opinion used to be a nice girl. God originally gave her life, breath and health. She went to Sunday School, prayed, and honored God with her life.

Jen: What went wrong?

Coach: The strangest thing happened. The liberals told her God's Word was not true. Then her existential friends told her she had to live for her experiences and her humanist teachers said she must measure up to man, not God. On top of that, the hedonist media convinced her to go for the gusto because she would only go around once.

Jen: Wow! What happened then?

Coach: She had an affair with Majority Rule, Sr. and became pregnant.

Jen: My gosh! What next?

Coach: Majority Rule Jr. was born, and you read about him last week. His conscience is almost gone.

Jen: Whatever happened to Public Opinion?

Coach: The last I heard, she was on drugs, was trillions in debt, had an abortion and finally got a year and seven months in prison for murdering a cop and is expected to be out in sixty days for good behavior. But she contracted AIDS and is not expected to live out the year.

Jen: What a drama! Whatever happened to Majority Rule Jr.? Is there any hope to change him?

Coach: Most likely. But he has one chance.

Jen: What's that?

Coach: I overheard his creator say, "If My people... shall humble themselves and pray and seek My face, and turn from their wicked ways, then I shall hear from heaven and will forgive their sin and will heal their land."

Closing Prayer:

Dear Lord, we know that our country is turning to the dark side more and more. Forgive us for not humbling ourselves, praying, and seeking Your face for our country, for surely, You gave us a great land, and we pray for Your mercy upon it. Amen.

Truth Theme: That's what will happen if we don't pray and obey our God.

coach@chapelfield.org

CHAPEL TALK
25
Who Are You Saved From?

"Let the nations now rejoice: Jesus saves!
Shout salvation full and free; highest hills and
deepest caves; this our song of victory:
Jesus saves!"

"We Have Heard the Joyful Sound,"
Priscilla J. Owens

WHO ARE YOU SAVED FROM?

Background: We had a discussion in theology class one day when a Roman Catholic student asked, "Christians are always talking about being saved. What are they being saved from?" I thought the best way to answer the question was with a short story.

When I was a boy in 1941, I was driving with my father in the farm country of northern New Jersey and listening to the car radio. It was about noon when all of a sudden, my dad pulled over and turned the radio up so that we could hear it better. We were just in time to hear the announcer say that Japanese bombers had attacked our naval base at Pearl Harbor. It was Sunday, December 7, and I was six years old.

Harrowing stories of that disaster began to come in; I remember one most clearly. It seems that a sailor on the battleship *Arizona* (on which over 1100 men died in that attack) was considered an outcast by his fellow crew members. Arrogant and obnoxious, he broke all the rules and, worst of all, he disappeared in times of trouble. He was labeled a coward by the crew. When the bombs started to fall that Sunday morning, this sailor headed aft toward the back of the ship, away from danger, rather than seeking to help his shipmates. Suddenly, an explosion occurred near him, and he was blown overboard. He landed a few hundred feet from the ship with broken ribs and two dislocated shoulders; unable to use his arms, he was forced to tread water with his feet only.

On top of that, he drifted into an oil slick that ignited. On all counts, he was a goner. He survived for a few hours as the fire moved closer to him. Just when he had lost all hope, a lifeboat bearing two sailors appeared through the smoke and approached him. One sailor recognized him and hollered to his companion, "Let's go pick someone else up!" The injured man yelled, "Help me! I can't swim! I am sorry! I am sorry!"

The first sailor repeated that they should move on to find another man to save. "He's no good anyway!" But the other sailor reached out and pulled the wounded man into the boat, and he was saved.

Pearl Harbor
December 7, 1941

My question to you students, is what was it that almost killed the sailor? Was it the explosion? Was it the fuel oil? Was it the fire? Or the angered sailor who wanted to leave him to his fate? What was it that would have killed him?

There was dead silence from the class. Then one hand went up in the back of the room. I recognized the student, and he said, "The water." Nodding, I answered, "You are right. The explosion, the oil, the fire, and even the sailor would not finish him off. It would be the water that would finally get him. He would drown."

Kids, the water is God, and the compassionate sailor is Jesus Christ. God, the judge, is the greatest killer of all mankind, and God in Jesus Christ is the greatest Savior of His people of all time. "The wages of sin is death," we read in Romans 6:23. Since all have sinned, all are under the death sentences. But Romans continues, "The gift of God is eternal life through Jesus Christ our Lord."

So, students, we are all downing, not because of the explosion, not because the oil or fire is gaining on us, but because we have broken the rules, the laws of God; our arms are broken, we cannot save ourselves. But Christ, like the second sailor, comes and saves all who yell, Help! For those who believe—even arrogant, obnoxious cowards—the boat coming alongside of them can save them, if they cry, "I am sorry, I repent."

That is why people who have repented and believed say they're saved. That is what we in this school and our churches want—for all our families, friends and neighbors to believe in Jesus Christ, repent and be saved from the righteous judgment of God. That is the gospel. Are you saved?

Closing Prayer:

Oh, God, let not the waters of Your judgment drown us. Help us cling to the lifeboat of Jesus Christ. May we not be rebellious or obstinate. Our arms are broken, we cannot swim to safety. Hear our cry for help. Give us the courage to say we are truly sorry for sins against Your holy name. Send Jesus Christ to save us. Amen

Truth Theme: God is the greatest killer of all mankind. Why? Because man has rejected the loving Savior He has provided. If you are drowning in the sea of rejection, cling to Him. The fire is approaching.

coach@chapelfield.org

CHAPEL TALK
26

Johnny No-Dids–
Johnny Yes-Did Nots

*"But let your yea be yea and let your nay
be nay, lest ye fall into condemnation."*

James 5:12

A Thought for Today

JOHNNY NO-DIDS—JOHNNY YES-DID NOTS

Background: Due to circumstances, I had less than ten minutes to do this chapel.

I think you all heard the expression, "your word is your bond." Kids, if you can't be trusted to do what you say, you will not only have few friends, but you also will not have a job for very long. Always do what you say, show up on time and keep your commitments, or if you can't, call to explain why. If you don't, your character will be destroyed. No one will trust you anymore.

When we first decided to open Chapel Field, I had the shell of the building up but didn't have rooms or the floor in it yet. The floor would be very expensive, and I didn't have the money. I was getting nervous as it was only a few months before we wanted to open. An answer to prayer was a good friend, Dr. Gene Gill, a local veterinarian, who volunteered to pay for the floor—over $3,000. But it would have to be done by the Friday of that week. Great, but I had to get the plumbing done for the bathrooms and kitchen before the cement could be poured. I now had two days to get it done. I called two plumber friends. One said he could not do it. The other said he would be here the next day at 7:00 a.m. sharp. I stopped worrying. By 11:00 a.m. the next morning, he still had not shown. I was in despair. The concrete was due to show up at 9:00 a day and a half later. Just when I was going to call him, the first plumber that I called showed up! He said, "I knew you were in a jam, so I changed my work schedule."

Kids, in Matthew 21:28, Jesus tells us in one of his shortest parables, the importance of this lesson. It's about "Johnny

No-dids" and "Johnny Yes-did nots":

A certain man had two sons, and he came to the first and said, 'Son, go work today in my vineyard.' He answered him and said, 'I will not.' But afterward, he repented and went. And he came to the second and said likewise. And he answered and said, 'I will go, sir,' and went not. Whether of the two did the will of his father?" They said unto Him, "The first." Jesus said unto them, "Verily I say unto you that the publicans and harlots go into the kingdom before you."

Students, keep your commitment to your parents, your school, your boss, your friends and most of all, to God. It's far better to say, no, you can't, than to say yes and not show up. It will define your character and represent who you are for the rest of your life. Be a "Johnny No-dids" before you are a "Johnny Yes-did nots"

Closing Prayer:

Oh, Father, we want to do Your will. Help us to carefully contemplate our words of commitment. Help us not to rashly make a commitment that we cannot keep. Help us to carefully evaluate the requests made to us that we may do Your will every opportunity we are given, so to be pleasing in Your sight. Amen.

<u>Truth Theme:</u> A man is only as good as his word.

P.S.–When I was in the hospital in 2016, one of my former students from 1986, George Comacho, visited me said, "Coach, do you remember that chapel you did 'Johnny No-Dids, Johnny Yes-Did Nots'? I think about that every time I make a commitment." I thought, Wow! Words speaking the truth really last!

coach@chapelfield.org

CHAPEL TALK
27
Your Bible:
Who is the Jesus of It?
(There is a Bully in School)

"Jesus Christ was one divine person in two natures, one human and one divine."

Council of Chalcedon, 451 AD

"Jesus is Kurios"

The early church

A Thought for Today

YOUR BIBLE: Who Was the Jesus of It?
(There is a Bully in School)

Background: Because of various discussions going on with our students about the Bible (at the time I was teaching four levels—Old Testament, theology, church history, and apologetics) I decided to do a three-chapel series on "Your Bible." First, who was the Jesus of it? Secondly, is there power in its words? And third, can you defend your Bible?

Students, over the next three chapels, I want to talk to you about your Bibles. Firstly, I want to ask you, can you trust your Bible? For example, is Jesus Christ who He said He was and is He able to deliver on the promises He made regarding having your sins forgiven, final salvation and eternal life? That's the question at stake on this issue. Secondly, is the Bible powerful enough or effective enough to make these promises come true in your life? And thirdly, can you or will you defend your Bible against false teaching?

First, can you believe what the Bible says about the one who claims He can give you eternal life? In other words, kids, is this Christ really divine (God), able to deliver on these promises, or simply a good man with moral suggestions? Many in the early church and in "churches" today believe Jesus is and was just a good, moral human being.

So, I want to tell you a story on how this problem of who Jesus really is has affected the church down through the ages. You know, kids, schools often have bullies. Bullies continue their obnoxious behavior until someone has the courage to stand up and confront them. I went to high school with a kid named Kenny. He was a great kid and a friend to most of us. He was a short kid and a little bit "nerdy," with his large glasses, but he was a real nice kid. Well, we had a bully in our class. Ricky was a pain in the butt to most everyone and he seemed to pick on Kenny the most. All of us guys told Ricky to lay off of Kenny. One day it came to a head. It seemed that Ricky was sitting right behind Kenny in History class. Ricky took his pencil point and ran it up the hair on the back of Kenny's neck. He did this over and over again. Kenny would jerk his head and tell Ricky to stop. Finally, at one point, Kenny couldn't take it anymore. He yelled out some expletives, got up and started flailing at Ricky in a rage. Ricky was still in his desk and couldn't get up! And Kenny was all over him. Well, the tussle lasted about two minutes and when it was over, Ricky had a bloody nose. Both boys got suspended from school but Ricky didn't bother Kenny any longer.

I am telling you this story because the same thing happened to the church of our Lord Jesus Christ three times since Jesus walked on the earth over 2,000 years ago and the response by the church was just the same as Kenny's. But the bully, Satan, kept trying to torment the church over and over again.

Kids, the first time Satan picked on the church was shortly after Jesus was resurrected and ascended to the throne of God. Between 100 A.D. and 450 A.D., the bully Satan tried to split the church by raising up false teachers (Arianism, Nestorianism, among others) who claimed that Jesus was not God). Some said He was not a man, just a "hologram," this because there was a common thought at that time, which stemmed from the Greek philosophers, that matter was evil; so how could Jesus being God take on a human (material) body? However, if Jesus were not also fully man, a lamb "without spot," how could he die for our sins?

The Gospel was at stake. So, three "Kennys" rose up to punch that bully Satan in the nose. The first "Kenny" was the creeds and councils of the early church. It began with the Apostles' Creed. Later, at the first Council of Nicea in 325 A.D., the early church fathers produced the Nicene Creed, which stated in part that Jesus was "*homoousios*" with the Father—"the same substance" as God. And in 451 A.D., the Council of Chalcedon settled the matter by asserting that Jesus was perfectly man and perfectly God. The council further confirmed that Jesus was consubstantial with God—"of one substance with the Father" and that He was God-man, "without confusion, without change, without division, without separation." This punched that bully out for about 1,000 years.

Satan next bullied the church by attacking the *message* of Jesus Christ—the Gospel of grace—by creating the institutionalism of the Roman Catholic religion. In Roman Catholic theology, you are saved according to your merits (which earn you eternal life), by enduring physical suffering in purgatory, and by worshiping the saints of old, rather than purely by the sovereign grace of God and by faith alone on the part of the believer. The second great "Kenny," the Reformers, rose up in the 1500s to punch out this distortion of truth generated by Satan. Martin Luther stated, from Scripture, that "Man is justified by faith, without the deeds of the law" (Romans 3:28). And further, "For by grace are you saved through faith and that not of yourselves, it is the gift of God, not of works," or merits. John Calvin wrote his wonderful *Institutes*, ending this matter, at least, theologically.

The third time that this bully Satan tormented Christ's church was on both the issues of the nature of Jesus (God or man) and Christ's Gospel of grace alone. This time, the bully used "scientific atheism." This false teaching came to America from Europe, and later from England, in the early 1900s. Known to us as "modernism" or liberalism, it claimed that Jesus was not divine (God) but simply a man, a good teacher whose practical lessons would make us better people. Church denominations such as the United Presbyterian, Episcopalian, and Methodist were most affected by this heresy and are now little more than social clubs. Later, Arminian-dispensationalism came with heresies that disclaimed the sovereignty of God over His creation and over our salvation. The third great "Kenny" rose up to knock this bully out—theologians like Charles Spurgeon, George Whitefield, Jonathan Edwards, and in our day, J. Gresham Machen, B.B. Warfield, J.I. Packer, R.C. Sproul and many others. Kids, I want you to know the names of these great "Kennys" down through the ages. They are great heroes of our faith. They will inspire you also as they have done for me and for many others.

Kids, I want to stop here. In this progression of false teachings and defenders of the truth in the Bible, stop to ask, as some of you are thinking, why are you going over this, Coach? This is not a church history class! I would say, do you trust the chair you are sitting on to support you? Do you trust the plane that you are going to see Grandma on to get you there safely? Why do you trust these things? Because the manufacturer abided by the laws of engineering and integrity in these products. So why would you trust the Bible to get you to ultimate safety—eternal life—if you did not have confidence in its integrity and the man who promised it? Hundreds of men have risked their lives and even died to guarantee you that our biblical theology is free from false teachings. The apostle said that the word of God will make you "wise unto salvation." What greater treasure could you have? Cling to it in this world of crisis. Live it. Trust in it and in the Christ it reveals—truly God, able to fulfill all of His promises to you. It is trustworthy.

I am going to talk with you next chapel about how my fellow Marine and I were transformed by the power of the words contained in your Bible and mine.

Closing Prayer:

Oh God, You have given us Your Word, proved by Your Holy Spirit, and defended by Spirit-guided men. Forgive us for not treasuring it as much as our iPhones. From its words, we know and can trust in Jesus Christ to fulfill His promises to give eternal life to all who believe. Amen.

Truth Theme: Your Bible, given by the Holy Spirit and defended by Spirit-filled men, is trustworthy for you to have the confidence to surrender your life to Jesus Christ.

coach@chapelfield.org

CHAPEL TALK

28

Your Bible:
Is There Power in Its Words?

*"But we all, with open face beholding
as in a glass the glory of the Lord,
are changed into the same image."*

2 Corinthians 3:18

YOUR BIBLE: Is There Power in Its Words?

Kids, last week we saw how false teachers tried to destroy the divinity of Jesus. This would make Him only a good, moral human being, meaning that His words had no power to fulfill the promise He made to give eternal life to those who believe. Thank God, great men rose up to exegete (bring out) the real Jesus of the Bible—*homoousia*—"of one substance with the Father, very God of very God;" totally capable of the power to fulfill His promises. This week I want to talk with you about the power of the Bible.

When I was a senior in high school, just like all of you in the back row, the Korean War was going on. One day while I was in English class, all the senior boys were called down to the gym. An army recruiter was waiting there. He told us that unless we joined some branch of service, we would be drafted into the army in thirty days. So, my friends and I decided to join the Marine Corps. Boot camp in 1954 was extremely demanding and at times, horrible (you can read about my boot camp experiences in my book, *The Obstacle Course*, MindStir Media, 2018). There I met a fellow Marine, Bob Hoppe, and we became good friends. After we completed boot camp and a couple of assignments, both Bob and I were transferred to the *USS Boston*, a guided missile cruiser, I as the admiral's security assistant and driver and Bob as a staff orderly.

Now Bob was a tough Marine. He would fight at the drop of an argument, could curse like a sailor, and drink most men under the table. One night when our ship was in port at Norfolk, Virginia, I had to go on an errand for the admiral. It was a rainy night, and Bob asked me to drop him off on East Main Street because he had liberty and wanted to go out drinking. I dropped Bob off, finished my errands and went back to the ship. At around four in the morning, Bob came in and began shaking me in my bunk. "Bill, wake up, wake up! I got saved tonight," he said. I was groggy but asked, "Saved from what?" "My sins," he replied. I told Bob, "You're drunk!" and guided him to his own bunk. He got down on his knees there, and at reveille (only two hours later), Bob was still on his knees.

Well kids, after I got Bob off his knees that morning, I never heard a cuss word come out of his mouth again. He never got into a fight again! He had a truly dramatic conversion! Later that day, I asked Bob what had happened the night before. He said that after I dropped him off, he had to walk a few blocks to where the bars were. On one corner there happened to be a youth group from a local church handing out Bible tracts. Bob had got in an argument with one member about some Bible issue (which Bob knew nothing about, however, he loved to argue about anything). The argument could not be settled, so the kids invited Bob to go to their pastor's home just down the block. That night, this pastor showed Bob in the Bible that he had sinned against God's holy laws and God's character. The pastor showed Bob in the Bible that the wages of his sin was death, and when he died, he must spend eternity in hell to pay for them. But the pastor said the gospel is that Jesus Christ has paid your debt on the cross and He offered eternal life if Bob would repent of his sins, believe God raised Jesus from the dead, repent in his heart and commit to follow Him.

After about five hours of arguing, Bob gave in to the power of God's Word, the Bible. He repented of his sin, believed and trusted in Christ. Bob was saved from the judgment of God! Overnight he was transformed and started a new life. The only problem was that the next day our ship set sail for a six-month deployment to the Mediterranean. Bob had no pastor he could talk to, no Christian friend that would help him with his new-found faith. All he had was a little 2½ inch x 3-inch pocket New Testament that we were given in boot camp and me.

Now, I was Roman Catholic, so I suggested that Bob go see the ship's chaplain who was a priest. So, he did, every night while we crossed the Atlantic. Every night he would come back shaking his head. Finally, I asked, "What's the matter, Bob?" He told me, "I am reading my New Testament every day, and the priest tells me to do things that are not in it. He never refers to the Bible. I don't think he believes the Bible. He says to pray to Mary, and he gave me a rosary. But the Bible says not to make vain repetitions. The priest says I have to go to confession so he can forgive my sin, but the Bible says there is one Mediator between God and man that can forgive sins and its Jesus Christ."

That got me thinking, so I began studying the little Bible with Bob. One night, sitting in the back seat of the admiral's car on the O-2 deck (the car was tied down on the second deck), over the choppy waters of the Mediterranean Sea, Bob led me to the Lord, and I accepted Christ by faith alone as my personal Savior.

So, look at what was done here. A faithful youth group, a faithful pastor, spoke the powerful word of God to Bob. The Holy Spirit taught Bob through a little, almost forgotten, New Testament word of God to sustain him in a desolate time at sea. Bob used the word of God to prove to me that I couldn't lean on my church or tradition or my own efforts to gain salvation.

So, what happened? What were the results of these experiences? Bob went on to college, graduated, got married and went out as a missionary to share the gospel with Mayo Indians high in the mountains of Colombia, South America. I went on to college, graduated, got married and went to the inner city to share the gospel with teens. The result was this high school where you are seated today, a school with over six hundred graduates that every day pledged to "live always, in His presence, under His authority and for His glory, *Coram Deo.*"

What does that say about the Bible? Unchanged, "it is the power of God unto salvation." Its message is that man can be saved unto eternal life. All of us must protect its integrity. The only thing between you and your natural destiny—hell—is the word of God, the Bible, that teaches the gospel with the power to save you. Because of the defenders of these words, who often gave their lives for the truth of it, you can trust your Bible. Next chapel time that I am with you I am going to tell you what attacks on the Bible are happening now. These will be your battles, to protect the power in the word of God.

Closing Prayer:

Oh God, if we are Christian, if we have responded to Your call of repentance and faith, it is only because someone explained Your Word to us. Without it, we would be lost. Thank you, Father, that with it we have the gospel of our Lord, Jesus Christ, and eternal life. Amen.

Truth Theme: The power of your Bible, the Gospel, will regenerate you and impute to you the righteousness of Christ Himself. Now that's power!

coach@chapelfield.org

CHAPEL TALK

29

Your Bible: Will You Defend It?

"But sanctify the Lord God in your hearts: and be ready always to give an answer to every man that asketh you a reason of the hope that is in you."

1 Peter 3:15

YOUR BIBLE: Will You Defend It?

Our scripture for this morning is found in Hebrews 4:12:

> *For the word of God is quick and powerful and sharper than a two-edged sword.*

I am going to refer to this verse later in this chapel. The two questions I asked you earlier were, first, can you trust your Bible? In that, we saw how false teachers sought to take the God out of Jesus thereby undermining the gospel of salvation by grace and faith alone. All of us are thankful for the great men that rose up to defend the biblical Jesus, "very God of very God," so that we could trust the truth of the gospel.

Secondly, I asked you, is there power in your Bible? Well kids, why did I ask you this? We saw that the Bible is not only doctrine. It is doctrine, but doctrine with a purpose. Its purpose is to give us a new experience, a new life, one of joy, righteousness, and mission. There is power in its words. That was demonstrated in the lives of two Marines who were isolated on the high seas and who only had a little New Testament.

Now I am going to ask you, can you defend your Bible? You might say to me, "Coach! I am not a theologian or a scholar. I can't defend the Bible!" I say, you can! And it's very important that you do. Why? Because in our day, attacks on the Bible are not on the nature of Jesus but on His message—His words (the final authority of the scriptures) and His message (the gospel of salvation by faith alone).

In the mid-1500s, this false teaching came to a head, affecting many, even up to today. Martin Luther was among the first to defend against these false teachings. He also stated that the Bible makes it clear that it is the final authority for faith and practice—not the pope or the Roman Catholic religion. This sent shock waves through the Vatican. Why? Because the popes had given themselves infallibility in their teachings. Then they ushered in such doctrines as saint worship, purgatory, and indulgences (payments to the church to ensure the release of loved ones from purgatory, essentially paying for their salvation).

Luther argued that this is not what the gospel teaches. First of all, Luther pointed out that the Bible is divinely inspired revelation right from the mouth of God Himself (2 Timothy 3:16). As far as the gospel was concerned, Luther showed that the Bible states, "For by grace are ye saved through faith, and this not of yourselves, not of works" (effort or merit). That sent daggers through the heart of infallibility and the Roman Catholic teaching of works-salvation. This ushered in the Protestant Reformation.

Kids, in doing this, Luther gave us two important principles that will make you without excuse if you don't think you are scholarly enough to defend your Bible? He gave us the principle of the perspicuity of scripture, which means that biblical truth is clear and understandable even to the common man. So, you don't have to be a scholar to defend and interpret your Bible.

Next, he said that the Bible speaks to us in anthropomorphic language, meaning in man's form—common, everyday language; words mean what they say. So, when the Bible says, "the Red Sea divided" and Israel walked on "dry land," that's just what happened. They didn't walk over a swamp, getting their feet wet as false teachers say. Why do they say this? Because they don't want to believe in divine intervention (miracles). Words mean what they say, especially in the doctrinal and historical books of the Bible. Other books like Psalms, Proverbs, some of the prophets, and Revelation use figures of speech, allegory and symbolic language that may require interpretation but not doctrinal, narrative or the historical books. They must be taken word for word as truth. Or could the virgin birth, the atonement, and the resurrection be whisked away as legend also?

In our day, there are many biblical truth battles to be fought. There is the origin of the universe. I will defend that issue in an upcoming chapel. There is a battle now among Christians also—how old is the earth? Was it created over billions of years ago as the scientists say or over seven twenty-four-hour days as the Bible says? Scientists say that carbon dating is evidence of an old-age earth theory. Many Christians believe this proposed theistic evolution (God created the universe over a long period of time). But what do the words in Genesis 1 mean, clearly mean? We know that Genesis is historical narrative and statements there must be considered fact, including where God said in Genesis 1, "And the evening and the morning were the first day." Any kindergartener knows that means one day. And Martin Luther's principle says that words mean clearly what they say. So, what is our argument to defend this scripture?

If I had the attention of these theistic evolution theory theologians, I would ask them three questions. Do you believe that Adam was created out of the dust of the earth? Most would say yes. Next, I would ask about how old he was when God created him. Most would probably say, in his teens because God said that he and Eve were to be fruitful and multiply. So, I would say, you believe that Adam was created with age? The answer must be yes! So, it was possible that God created the universe with age?

Kids, words mean clearly what they say. If we are not careful, the words *incarnation*, *resurrection*, and *atonement* will be labeled incorrect also. You can and must defend your Bible, to your friends, in church, and to the world.

Your Bible is trustworthy in everything it says about Jesus. Your Bible is powerful, and your Bible is clear and understandable in its inspired words, able in its truth to provide salvation to all who believe. Trust it, experience its power, and defend its truth.

Closing Prayer:

Oh God, our Father, forgive us for not thanking You for the great treasure You have placed in our hands. Drive us to Your Word of life, so that it will consume us with its truth, leading us to eternal life and into Your service. Amen.

Truth Theme: Truth is worth defending. The Bible is truth. Don't shy away from defending it.

coach@chapelfield.org

CHAPEL TALK
30
You Be the Judge

"Hear the causes between your brethren, and judge righteously between every man and his brother, and the stranger that is with him."

Deuteronomy 1:16

A Thought for Today

YOU BE THE JUDGE

We all love to identify with our local teams; in New York, it's the Yankees or the Mets. In Chicago, it's the White Sox and the Bears. In St. Louis, it's the Cardinals, and so it goes. Well, in ancient Greece, it wasn't baseball or football; it was wrestling. Different cities—Athens, Corinth, and others—had wrestling teams that traveled from town to town to participate in matches. At most matches, teams showed up with an odd number of participants. Athens may have nine wrestlers and Corinth eight. The odd wrestler would be called upon, because he had no opponent, to pair the teams according to their height and weight. Then after the match, he counted the points for each team. Therefore, he was called the unpaired wrestler, meaning he couldn't pair himself with another wrestler.

In England, in the early 1900s, the term for the judge was renamed *umpire* for the game of cricket. Later, when baseball became popular, the name became synonymous with the men officiating America's pastime, not because the umpire had to pair players but because he had to count balls and strikes. He has to judge every pitch.

How important a judge is to all sports! He must judge whether the ball was caught in play or out of play, whether the runner was safe at first or not. If we didn't have umpires—officials to judge close plays—games would result in total chaos.

I remember when I was in college, we got enough men together to have a make-up baseball game. Everything was okay until there was a close play at home plate. An argument broke out and could not be settled. Tempers raged, and a fight broke out. That was it. We all had to go home in the second inning.

The Judge's decision is final

Judges are critical. Society cannot function without them. Police judge our driving behavior. Court judges have to determine civil and criminal matters. Why is this? Because we can't exist without being held accountable for our actions. Baseball players always want to be safe at first, whether the call turns out to be right or not! John Calvin said that it is part of human nature to see ourselves as right when we are actually wrong in the sight of the rules. What would happen if we left it up to a runner to determine if he were safe on first base or not? The score would be 100 runs to zero before the end of the first inning. Sports and society cannot function like that. It would be a disaster. This is what happened in Judges 21:25, "Every man did what was right in his own eyes."

Paul warns believers about this in 1 Corinthians 11:31, "For if we would judge ourselves, we should not be judged." In other words, judge yourself now before it's too late and if you find yourselves out (according to God's rules, His laws) and you are not safe like you wanted to be, you can avoid the penalty of hell by trusting in Jesus Christ who took the penalty for you on the cross. By judging yourself, you can be safe for all eternity. That is the gospel. You be the judge!

Closing Prayer:

Lord, we know life is not a game. If we need umpires to judge our behavior here, how much more will humanity need to be judged at Your return? Help us to judge ourselves now while there is time, confess our sins, accept Jesus as Lord and Savior now so that we can face Your final judgment in confidence, so that we may be safe for all eternity. Amen.

Truth Theme: The God of all eternity has judged you out at first! The only way you can make it home safely is "Christ in you, the hope of victory." Let Him bat for you.

coach@chapelfield.org

CHAPEL TALK

31

My Version of Rip Van Winkle

*"For by him were all things created, that
are in heaven, and that are in earth,
visible and invisible, whether they be thrones,
or dominions, or principalities, or powers:
all things were created by him, and for him."*

Colossians 1:16

A Thought for Today

MY VERSION OF RIP VAN WINKLE

<u>Background:</u> When I would get to the place with my students where we were discussing the origin of the universe, I would tell them my version of the story of Rip Van Winkle.

This morning, students, I want to tell you the story of Rip Van Winkle. He is a fictional character whose tale was set back in 1870. One day, he wanted to go out of town for a day's getaway. So, he hitched his old faithful horse Dan to his buckboard and went far into the countryside. That was the only mode of transportation in those days besides walking. While on his journey on a mid-summer afternoon, he saw a very large field and spotted a big apple tree right in the middle of it. He thought that it would be a nice place to take a nap and maybe there would be an apple there to have as a snack. So, he tied his old pal Dan to a tree branch and set off. When he got there, he found a good apple and settled down at the base of the tree to rest and enjoy his treat. The warmth of the sun and a mild breeze soon put him fast asleep.

Rip Van Winkle asleep under a tree

He woke up abruptly when a cloud went over the sun. Rubbing his eyes, he said, "I must get back to Ol' Dan. He may need a drink of water by now." However, what Rip Van Winkle did not know was that he had slept for a hundred years! It was now 1970. Not knowing this, he walked back to where Ol' Dan was tied up, his horse and his buckboard were gone! However, parked on the old country road where he left Dan was a very odd carriage. It had four wheels, just like his old buckboard but they had rubber wrapped around them. It had seats but no place to hook up a horse. He shook his head. What was this metal object anyway? It had an emblem on the front that said, Ford Mustang. What was this crazy-looking carriage?

Not knowing it, old Rip Van Winkle was looking at a brand-new Ford Mustang convertible! He sat in it. He pushed some buttons. Wow! The top went up! He didn't know it, but it had a 225-horsepower engine, a five-speed transmission, power steering, a hi-fi radio, even on and off headlamps that you didn't have to light with a match. What was this crazy contraption?

Rip looked up, and a man was taking a stroll down this back country road on that warm afternoon. Rip ran up to the man. Startled, the man asked, "Who are you?" (By this time, Rip had a very long beard and very out-of-date clothing.) He said, "I am Rip Van Winkle, good sir. Who are you?" The man replied, "I am Dr. Harry Jones. I am a scientist." Rip said, "Dr. Harry, please tell me, what is this object here on the side of the road and where did it come from?" The scientist said, "It's a car, and it came from a big explosion which put it all together." Rip thought for a minute and said to himself, "This guy is crazy. I'll go to my farmer friend to explain who built this contraption." Why did Rip think like that? Because even a man born in 1840 and a farmer knows that **complexity demands a designer**. Rip knew that even a simple buckboard had to have an engineer to figure it out.

So, kids, when you go to college and sit in biology class, and they tell you that all the complexities of the universe, including your human body, came from a **Big Bang**, just think of Ol' Rip—you can't put nothing over on me! I'll take the truth from a simple farmer. Complexity demands a designer. But that's what they will tell you in the highest circles of academia. It all started with a **Big Bang**. Let's examine this theory for a minute.

Student: Where did this Big Bang come from?

Teacher: From energy.

Student: Where did the energy come from?

Teacher: We don't know.

Student: Then is it possible it came from nowhere, out of nothing?

Teacher: Yes.

So, what do the scientists tell us? A Big Bang happened out of nowhere and produced the (Mustang) complexities we see around us! These scientists and your college professors deny their own principle of cause and effect, which states that every effect must have a cause. Kids, if there ever was nothing, there would be nothing now! The Big Bang happening out of nothing is magic, not science. It's the self-creation argument. It just couldn't be possible for something to create itself. It would have to exist before it was. Stick with Rip Van Winkle on this. These scientists are crazy, not using their intelligence and surely not common sense.

The Bible gives us a more valid answer. In its first five words, it says, "In the beginning God created." At least in this statement, we have something, and we know that out of something, something can come; out of nothing, nothing can come.

So students, please don't be embarrassed that you are a Christian when you find yourself in the college classroom. You believe in God by pure reason; they believe in their theory by magic. However, belief that God sent Jesus Christ into His created world to save sinners, is by faith. This is why the prophet Isaiah said, "Come now, and let us reason together, saith the LORD: though your sins be as scarlet, they shall be as white as snow;" (Isaiah 1:18). The scientist can't examine what is behind this dimension and the power that is there, but they can examine this creation that the psalmist says, "declares the glory of God" and they are responsible for acknowledging the God that reveals Himself there and the Christ they reject.

So, kids, don't let anybody fool you. Be proud of your God. He is both the designer-creator and redeemer of your world and life. Remember Rip Van Winkle.

Closing Prayer:

Oh Lord Jesus, You said in Your Word that our minds should be stayed on Thee. There only can we find peace in a totally unreasonable world. Help us to use our minds, energy, and all of our faith in the battle for presenting Jesus Christ to our world. Amen.

Truth Theme: God uses the foolish things of this world to confound the wise. What is foolish to the intellectuals is very reasonable to the Christian.

coach@chapelfield.org

CHAPEL TALK

32

Don't Read This Chapel Talk!

*"Let goods and kindred go,
this mortal life also."*

"A Mighty Fortress," Martin Luther

A Thought for Today

DON'T READ THIS CHAPEL TALK!
(It May Endanger Your Lifestyle)

Background: I could not give this talk to our general student body. I gave it to Youth Conquest with Christ, our Christian service fraternity. These are students who had committed to serve God with their lives. The question came up, "How can I be a disciple?"

I can answer that question, kids, by asking you a question. How much faith do you have? Notice, I am asking you, how much faith. I am not asking you whether you have faith or not. I know that if you are a Christian, you had to exercise faith in who Jesus was and in His resurrection from the dead. But I am asking how much faith.

God sets the bar for salvation quite low—simply believe and be saved. However, the bar for discipleship is very high. How high? Listen to these words of Jesus. In Luke 14:33, Jesus says, "Whoever does not forsake all that he has cannot be My disciple." The Amplified Bible says, "So then, any of you who does not forsake (renounce, surrender claim to, give up, say goodbye to) all that he has cannot be My disciple." Also, Jesus said in Matthew 19:21, "If you would be perfect, go and sell what you have and give to the poor... to be My disciple" (AMP). Jesus went further in Mark 8:34-35. Listen to what happened there, "Then he called the crowd to him along with his disciples and said: 'If anyone would come after me, he must deny himself and take up his cross and follow me. For whoever wants to save his life will lose it, but whoever loses his life for me and for the gospel will save it.'" (Mark 8:34-35, NIV). The apostle Paul reinforced this declaration of Jesus, "I beseech you therefore, brethren, by the mercies of God, to present your bodies a living sacrifice, holy, acceptable to God, which is your spiritual service" (Romans 12:1, ASV).

The bar is set very high for you to get over if you want to be a disciple of Jesus. (You can read about my confrontation with this issue in my book, *The Obstacle Course*, chapter 13.) You will need to have a lot of faith to get over this bar. It depends on how much you want it and how much you want to please your Savior.

Jesus further adds pressure to this proclamation: If you do want to follow Me (be a disciple), know this, "the foxes have holes and birds have nests, but the Son of Man has nowhere to lay His head" (Luke 9:58). And further added these dreadful words: "No man having put his hand to the plow and looking back is fit for the Kingdom of God."

Now you know why I asked you how much faith you have. As a young person confronted with this truth, you need to plan your future very carefully. If you are married, have children and a job, when you are confronted with certain realities, you will have to make some big decisions. This was my situation when I was confronted with the cost of discipleship. I had a wife, four children, a small farm (mortgage-free), I had a lot of farm equipment there and a garage for all of them. I had two airplanes, one for fun, short trips and a twin-engine for long distance trips. I had a motorcycle, a boat and I had a barn full of exotic cows, and in my barn, a 1957 Ford Thunderbird which I was in the process of restoring. I had a swimming pool for the kids and a good paying job that allowed me plenty of time to do everything. Wow! And Jesus said, if you would be My disciple, "sell what you have, give to the poor, take up your cross and follow Me," and then the added words, you will have no place to lay your head.

Well, kids, I had no other choice. I couldn't look back. That wasn't an option. So, I sold everything—the planes, the motorcycle, the boat and cows, the Thunderbird. I kept only two cars, the house, and the property, gave to the poor (a family of Laotian refugees), sought to sell my house and property so I could look for a place that our family could serve the Lord (you can also read about this in *The Obstacle Course*).

At that time, I learned a very big lesson. I was trying to follow the Lord's command to sell what you have. I tried to sell the farm over and over again. One day while I was looking out my window at my beautiful piece of property, God spoke to my mind and said, "Don't give Me what you want to give Me, give Me what you've got." That ultimately produced the chairs you are sitting in right now. Although human, I never looked back.

One day, my wife told me a nationally known evangelist was going to speak at a local church. We decided to go. He was speaking about the cost of discipleship. In the course of his message, he said, "If you are truly committed to God, you must give everything over to Him—your car, your family, your money, everything. And God sees that you are willing and then He gives it all back to you." I felt my wife tugging on my trousers. I wanted to stand up and yell, "No, no. Wrong, wrong. He won't give it back to you!" When you give everything that you possess over to God, He never ever gives it back to you! What He does do, however, is make you the manager of what are His assets. You now manage for Him what was once yours, and He will give back to you only what's needed for you to survive as His manager of His vineyard. Now it's not just a ten-percent tithe but 100% of everything. That's what the apostle Paul meant when He said, "You are not your own; you are bought with a price."

So, kids, you still want to be a disciple? Count the cost. When you consider what Christ did for you at Calvary and what He offers you for eternity, the cost to you will seem insignificant. When I was a kid in 1942, just seven years old, I can remember vividly old Bill Decker, a worker on my dad's dairy farm, hooking his favorite draft horse to our one bottom plow (we had no tractors, gasoline, electricity or indoor plumbing out at the farm in those days). Between milking in the morning and milking every evening, Bill could plow about four acres. It was hard, walking one foot in the furrow and one on unplowed ground all day! But ol' Bill never looked back! He just plodded on! But it paid in big dividends when we ate sweet corn late in the summer and the milk checks, though small, kept coming in.

The cost of discipleship may be great, but the benefits of the harvest will be even greater. And you will be able to say you helped plow the field for the King of Kings and Lord of Lords.

Closing Prayer:

Oh Lord, when you bring us to that crossroad when we must decide to be your disciple, teach us the truth of Martin Luther's words: "Let goods and kindred go; this mortal life also" and guide our understanding to willingly be Your disciples. Amen.

Truth Theme: When you consider true discipleship, if you really want it and are single, sacrifice your life to Christ and His cause. If you are married, sacrifice your future and be a profitable manager of all of what He has given you.

coach@chapelfield.org

CHAPEL TALK
33
Keep Your Head in the Cockpit

"Thy word is a lamp unto my feet"
"I trust in Thy word."

Psalm 119:105b, 42b

KEEP YOUR HEAD IN THE COCKPIT

Kids, I am sorry for using so many aviation illustrations in my chapel times. However, there is so much in my flying experiences that bring out biblical truths that I cannot resist in telling them. When I was a flight instructor, one of my students was Brian Barns. At the airport, we called him B.B. He had a great personality. I got B.B. soloed. (Soloed is when a student pilot has learned enough to make takeoffs and landings by himself.) I got out of the plane and B.B. completed three good takeoffs and landings by himself, then he had officially soloed. At that point, I let one of my top flight instructors, Dave Marcino, take him on to get Brian ready to solo cross-country and then to prepare for his private pilot flight test. As part of that preparation, each student must spend at least two hours "under the hood." This means he would wear a hood that restricted his vision to the instrument panel only. Why? Because each pilot must demonstrate that he is able to fly the plane on instruments without looking at any reference points outside, like the horizon (to keep yourself level) and other checkpoints. This is to make sure a pilot can fly the plane safely in hazy or bad weather. Why is this critical in his training? Because if you don't keep your eyes on the instruments and look out of the cockpit to see the horizon or other reference points, you will get vertigo (not knowing which way is up or down). You become completely disoriented as to which is up, down, left, or right. If a pilot then looks back at his instruments, he may not make sense of them and enter a spin and crash.

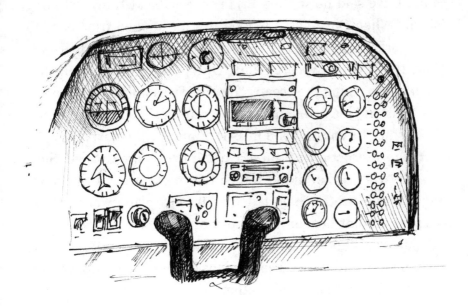

Private airplane instrument panel

If you get into this type of situation, all pilots say, "keep your head in the cockpit." Trust your instruments. In other words, keep your eyes on the instruments, fly the plane within its limits until you have a clear view of the horizon and ground reference points.

Back to Brian Barns, Dave and I got him his private pilot's license. He quickly bought a very nice used four-passenger airplane and immediately wanted to take his wife and two children flying on a long cross-country trip. I cautioned him to fly locally for a while so he could gain experience.

One hazy Sunday after church I was flying with a student in the pattern (just above the airport), shooting landings and takeoffs. Dave was also up with a student doing air work. I saw B.B. taking off with his family and noted it to Dave on the radio. Dave said he spotted Brian's plane headed toward Long Island. When Dave and I landed, we questioned friends as to where Brian was going. "To Martha's Vineyard," was the reply. Now, there were two problems. One was the haze intensifies when approaching the ocean. The other was Martha's Vineyard was an island located about twenty minutes' flying time off the Massachusetts coast. If you miss it, France is the next stop.

As the afternoon went on, Dave and I got more worried. Sure enough, when Brian didn't return that night, we got the news. Flight Service radar reported that Brian's plane went off the radar at a point headed way south of the Vineyard. Brian, his wife, and his children were never found. I was very grieved. If we had known that was Brian's plan, I would have stopped him from going in that kind of weather.

The lessons I learned from this tragedy were, keep your head in the cockpit, obey your instruments. Let them be your guide. The scriptures are our instruments. Keep your eyes fixed on them, understand them. Learn about them, trust in them. The psalmist wrote, "Thy word have I hid in my heart that I might not sin against thee" (Psalm 119:11). I might add, "Doing this, you won't get vertigo, crash and burn." Solomon also advised us, lean not on your own understanding, acknowledge Him in all your ways and He will get you safely out of the haze.

Closing Prayer:

Oh, Father, help us not to get disoriented in our flight of life. You have given us the instruments to fly safely home. May we trust the scriptures and not get disoriented by the distractions of our cul-

ture. Help us to keep our heads focused in the cock-
pit. Amen.

Truth Theme: Thy word is a lamp unto my feet and a light to my flight path. It is the only way to prevent Christian vertigo.

coach@chapelfield.org

34

What's the Big Deal About the Reverse Rotten Apple Theory?

*"But ye are a chosen generation,
a royal priesthood, an holy nation,
a peculiar people; that ye should shew forth
the praises of him who hath called you out of
darkness into his marvellous light."*

1 Peter 2:9

A Thought for Today

WHAT'S THE BIG DEAL ABOUT THE REVERSE ROTTEN APPLE THEORY?

Kids, you have got to know this theory. It is the key to understanding your Bible and our Christian world and life-view. Go with me to Genesis 3. Man disobeyed God by wanting to know evil. "In the day you eat thereof then your eyes shall be opened, and ye shall be as God knowing good and evil." Go on to Genesis 4—Cain kills Abel. The first giant step in the outworking of evil. Next, let's go to Genesis 6. There, evil was infectious. "God saw that the wickedness of man was great in the earth and that every imagination of the thoughts of his heart was only evil continually" (Genesis 6:5). The consequence? "I will destroy man whom I have created from the face of the earth" (Genesis 6:7).

Enter Noah and his ark, saving only his family and representatives of all living creatures, both male and female. One year later, on Mount Ararat, Noah and his family leave the ark with all the creatures, big and small. At that point, God made two statements to Noah. One was a promise and one a command. In the promise, known as the Noahic covenant, God committed never to destroy the earth again with a flood (Genesis 9:11-17). But God also commanded Noah, "Be fruitful and multiply and replenish the earth" (Genesis 9:1). Wow! Noah was to be the founder of a new human race! What an honor and responsibility.

Now, Noah knowing that one rotten apple would spoil the entire basket and that he and all human beings were, at their hearts, sinful creatures, I believe Noah, very humbly and respectfully, asked God why, considering the Genesis 6 situation, would his future generations not become evil in every imagination of their hearts also? In other words, "God, will evil and wickedness not overwhelm humanity and prevail again?" I imagine the next conversation with Noah and God went something like this:

"Noah, you remember the Rotten Apple Theory?"

"Yes, Lord."

"I am going to institute the **Reverse Rotten Apple Theory**. I am going to put good apples in a rotten basket and through the power of My Holy Spirit, will change some rotten apples into good apples. You and your family will start this process. But I am going to officially give My promise to a guy named Abraham."

Basket of apples

So, kids, the Reverse Rotten Apple Theory became not a theory but a historical fact. God called these new apples the *church* (the *called-out ones*)—the people of God. These now were called to be good apples in a rotten basket. Their sin and the consequences thereof would be dealt with at the cross but for now, all those bad apples converted (born again) would have to trust (have faith) and obey their Savior. The Bible is the historical record of that process, the theme of which is "I will be your God, and you will be My people." This Reverse Rotten Apple Theory is clearly seen in 1 Peter 2:9-10:

> *[Y]e are a chosen generation, a royal priesthood, an holy nation, a peculiar people; that ye should shew forth the praises of him who hath called you out of darkness into his marvellous light; Which in time past were not a people, but are now the people of God."*

New apples now show forth Jesus Christ to all rotten apples in this world.

Now students, why is this Reverse Rotten Apple Theory so important to you? Because if you, by the Holy Spirit, have been given the faith to trust and believe God and are obedient to Him, you are a part of the greatest movement for good since the creation when history began. You have the privilege of being the means whereby bad apples are changed into good ones. You can be a co-worker with God in this glorious endeavor. What a privilege! You can be on God's team! God said to the first official good apple in the basket, Abraham, "Because of your faith in Me... in thee shall all the families of the earth be blessed" (Genesis 15:6, 12:3).

So, kids, when you look out upon this world—politics,

economy, society, and culture—you can see terrible evil, and you can see good. You know down deep in your heart what is really going on is good apples working at changing bad apples into good ones. The effect of this covenant with Abraham, "All the families of the earth will be blessed" is being fulfilled in front of your eyes. The trickle-down effect of good apples has given us the defense of freedom from despots in multiple wars, the benefits of science, industry, education, hospitals, technology, and democracy. This democracy is only good if the good apples and those influenced by it have the majority.

So, what's the big deal about the Reverse Rotten Apple Theory? Just the history of redemption and salvation and its influence fighting against the evil of Satan in this world, this leads to victory, ushering a new environment where there will be no evil, famine, hate, and disease. That is the big deal! The greatest deal of all! Be a part of it!

Closing Prayer:

Oh Lord, give us eyes to see and ears to hear what Your Word is trying to teach us, and grant us faith to trust and obey You so that we can be good apples in Your kingdom. Amen.

Truth Theme: You will either be an instrument to affect change in bad apples or be a friend to the evil empire. Be a part of the greatest story ever told—show Him forth!

coach@chapelfield.org

CHAPEL TALK
35
Are Tithes Still Required?

"We are either all in or not in at all."

Author, to his wife,
when he confronted discipleship

A Thought for Today

ARE TITHES STILL REQUIRED?

Kids, I have done chapel talks on this subject several times over the years. One notable one was called "Don't Read This Chapel Talk." However, I don't have much time this morning, so I will give you another slant on the subject.

We live in a Christian culture where clear distinctions are made between what is God's and what is mine. We give God one, perhaps two hours a week and reserve the other 166 for ourselves. We put some money in the collection plate, but according to national statistics, keep 96% for our own use. We have abilities and talents, but they rarely see use in the Kingdom of God. Though all our resources are given to us by God, we guard and protect them for ourselves carefully.

The New Testament knew nothing of this distinction. Jesus forever put to death the idea that there are "my things" and "God's things" during a conversation He had with a young man inquiring about attaining eternal life: "Go sell all your possessions and give to the poor... and come and follow Me" (Matthew 19:21). Jesus did not require ten percent and then an offering. He required 100% of that man's time, talents, and resources. I heard a nationally known speaker say, "Jesus did not mean that the young man had to give God all of his wealth. He was testing him to see if he was willing." Hogwash! Kids, Jesus meant every word He said. Give Him all or give Him nothing. In the parable of the talents, three servants (Christians) are called to give an account for the use of their resources. They did not say, "Master, here is 10%. Thanks for trusting me with your resource." They gave 100% plus the increase of what was entrusted to them back to their master—the *Kurios*—the Lord Jesus Christ.

Every Christian is entrusted with a life which equals time, talents, and resources. Jesus is clear, "If you save your life, you will lose it. If you lose your life for my sake and the gospel's you shall save it" (Mark 8:35). Paul is no less emphatic. "Present your bodies (time, talent, resources) a living sacrifice." Your life is not your own. There is a mission going on! The time is racing down. The gospel must be spread; the opportunity is great. Forget an hour a week; forget "tithes and offerings." That is for leisure time! Cast yourselves 100% into the battle. Make no distinctions. Throw in your money, your education, your time and serve the Lord of Lords—the King of Kings—with your life.

Closing Prayer:

Oh Lord, You want everything from us because You gave everything for us in Your life and death on the cross. Please help our minds to understand this critical truth. Give us strength to serve and an obsession for Your kingdom. Amen.

Truth Theme: You only have one life. It will quickly pass. Only what's done for Christ will last.

coach@chapelfield.org

CHAPEL TALK

36

The Student Honor Code Has Too Many Rules!

"Blessed are they that keep his testimonies, and that seek him with the whole heart."

Psalm 119:2

THE STUDENT HONOR CODE
HAS TOO MANY RULES!

Background: This comment came up in class one day when we were discussing the laws that God gave to Moses, so I did a brief chapel talk on the subject.

Kids, a student asked me, "Why does our student honor code have so many rules? Even my family feels that some are not that important." Please excuse me if I give a personal illustration. In my house, I have made it tough to be a Spanjer. One of my desires is that when my kids leave the nest, they will say, "Wow! That was tough. I am proud to be a Spanjer." Have we laughed and wrestled with each other? Yes. Have we hugged and encouraged each other? Yes. Have we marched in parades and participated in Little League and told each other, "I love you"? Yes. Have we relaxed our standards and expectations one degree? No!

Having worked with young people for forty years, I am overwhelmed by the fact that most Christian kids have no pride in Christianity. Many lack pride in themselves, their families, and their churches. Parents today do not demand the highest standard of behavior nor have great expectations of service for their kids. The result is a generation of Christians who live selfishly, without vision and without life of sacrifice and commitment to Christ and His kingdom.

STUDENT HONOR CODE

I will:

1. Tell the truth at all times and be respectful in word, manner and action to my parents, school staff and those in authority, and will not cheat or steal.

2. Use proper and inoffensive language; not smoke; not use alcoholic beverages outside of the church or family settings; not view or listen to entertainment material that is obscene or that promotes immorality.

3. Dress modestly, so as not to draw special attention to myself; be neatly groomed and comply with the school's dress code.

4. Obey all the laws of our land wherein they harmonize with the Word of God and be a testimony for Christ in word and deed, realizing that I am a reflection first of God, then of my family, school and church.

5. Strive to live in accordance with the Biblical teaching on sexuality, seeking to live a chaste and holy life to the glory of God.

6. Study diligently, striving for the highest academic excellence within my ability; give my best attention in class; complete all of my assignments and maintain the highest academic integrity.

7. Be considerate of my fellow students, helping and encouraging them in every way I can and refusing to participate in gossip.

8. Be faithful in my commitment to extra-curricular activities at Chapel Field and strictly obey their requirements.

9. Be faithful in my personal walk with Christ through my private devotions, church attendance and my Christian service.

10. Keep this code both in and out of school, by living my life always in the presence of God, under His authority and for His glory.

Coram Deo

CF student honor code

Having high standards and living up to great expectations is a result of keeping the rules. Living up to them creates character and pride in accomplishment. There is a false sense of pride that comes from an arrogant heart, puffed up with self-conceit—the kind, the Bible says, goes before a fall. But there is another kind of positive pride—the kind that caused God to say about His creative activity, "It is good!" or that caused Jesus to say, "It is finished." It caused Paul to say, "I press on," and Martin Luther to say, "Here I stand." This is the pride that gives us inner excitement of unspeakable joy when we know that, with God's help, we are living up to His expectations for us and that we are pleasing Him.

As a young Marine at Parris Island in '54, the rules were tough. Standards and expectations were high. We started with 130 men. In thirty days, there were seventy-five rule-keepers left. Rules were not optional. There was one for every moment of every day. At graduation, we were proud! Character was developed, and every one of us knew we made it by the grace of God! God does not relax His standards. We must demonstrate our love for Him with every action and serve Him with every breath (Matthew 22:37). If you keep the rules, you will be proud to be a Christian. You will attract enlistments. High standards! Great expectations!

Closing Prayer:

Oh, holy God, David said, "I love Your law, oh God." Teach us gently but at all costs that Your laws and the rules of our parents are meant to give us the character to be successful in life with You. Amen.

Truth Theme: Keeping rules is tough and a pain. But high standards develop discipline, and discipline, character. It will be your most valuable asset in life.

coach@chapelfield.org

CHAPEL TALK
37
God Cannot Forgive Your Sins...

"God has a big 'dilemma' that was solved before the foundation of the world."

R.C. Sproul, speaking on the atonement

A Thought for Today

GOD CANNOT FORGIVE YOUR SINS...

Background: This morning I observed my students were very sleepy and lethargic. I decided to shock their theological senses awake with my chapel talk title. This was also around the time that final exams were approaching, and I wanted to make sure they completely understood and could explain the cost of the atonement.

Good morning, students! You look bright and alert this morning so I want you to wrap your minds around this theological statement: God cannot forgive your sins. I'll say it again—**God cannot forgive your sins.** (All of the students woke right up and by their facial expressions, they thought I was a crazy heretic in a just-wait-till-I-tell-my-pastor kind of way. There was a lot of mumbling and whispering. I let it go on for a few minutes before continuing.)

Kids! You didn't let me finish my statement before you started groaning and moaning. I was telling you, God cannot forgive your sins... that are not paid for. God cannot give you mercy and forgiveness while you have an outstanding debt. Since you and I are created in God's image, when we sin, we reflect to others that God is like that also, that sin creates a debt we owe to God. He desires to be compassionate and loving to His creation and forgive our sin, but because He is righteous and holy, He cannot forgive a debt that is not paid. Therefore, He has a big dilemma. If God exercised His right hand of holiness, righteousness, and justice against our debt, we would die ("The wages of sin is death"—Romans 6:23). If on the other hand, God said to Himself, "I love man that I created, so I'll just forgive Him by exercising My compassion and love," He would cease to exist. Why? Because God is **righteous** and **just**; it's part of His nature, and He cannot be otherwise.

You see God's big dilemma—a very critical predicament. What could He do? It reminds me of a time when I was seven years old and in second grade. The war against Japan had been going on for about one year. Things were not going well for our side. General MacArthur had just escaped from Corregidor in the Philippines. Eleven thousand American troops had surrendered to the Japanese who forced the captives on a sixty-nine-mile long march, known as the Bataan Death March. Eighty thousand Filipino and American captives began the march—18,000 Filipinos and 500 Americans died along the way. They died from thirst, hunger and when they finally fell from exhaustion, their Japanese captors ran them through with their bayonets. When my second-grade class heard the news report, we were devastated. The memory of those events still haunts me to this day. I thought at that time (even though I was little), "How did this happen?" Years later I understood the reason. General Wainwright had a tough decision to make. His dilemma was either to fight until the last American soldier was killed, be pushed into the China Sea, or surrender. He chose to surrender to save the most men possible. This was a very sad day for all Americans.

The only relief I had in those days from the gloomy war news was the radio programs I listened to at 7:30 each night. There was "The Shadow Knows," "The Green Hornet," "Captain Midnight," and the one I liked most, "The Lone Ranger and Tonto." I remember one episode where the two got themselves behind some large rocks with high cliffs behind them and they were attacked by a fierce group of Indians. A real dilemma! They couldn't fight their way out, and they couldn't climb the high cliffs. I remember what the Lone Ranger said, "We are between a rock and a hard place, Tonto." The cavalry came to their rescue just in the nick of time, and they were saved.

This is the sort of dilemma God faced when confronted with man's sin. But God planned from all eternity not to surrender, not to go into the sea or hide behind the rocks. God sent the cavalry in to rescue mankind. He sent His Son Jesus to die on the cross in our place, and He paid our debt for us (*huper*). He was the propitiation, a substitute for us. That's the gospel. That's the good news. Our debt to God, which we could not pay ourselves is **paid in full**. When we were stuck with the ocean on one side, and high cliffs on the other and the enemy (Satan) was ready to kill us, God saved us by His pure grace alone. We didn't have to go on any death march or climb any cliffs.

[See following diagram]

The Trinity
Father - Son - Holy Spirit
"God"

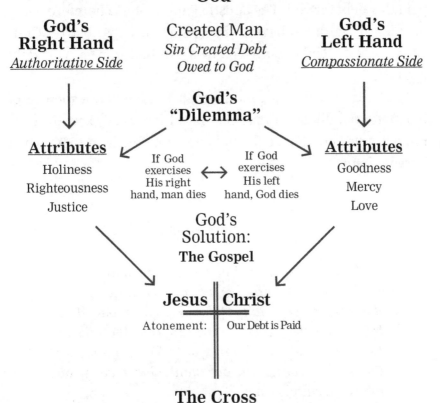

God's Right Hand	Created Man	God's Left Hand
Authoritative Side	*Sin Created Debt Owed to God*	*Compassionate Side*

God's "Dilemma"

Attributes

Holiness
Righteousness
Justice

If God exercises His right hand, man dies ⟷ If God exercises His left hand, God dies

Attributes

Goodness
Mercy
Love

God's Solution:
The Gospel

Jesus ‖ Christ
Atonement: Our Debt is Paid

The Cross
Brings Both Attributes Together — Satisfies the Dilemma

"Justified by faith, we have peace with God." Romans 5:1

Graphic design: Andy Spanjer

The cross united God's holiness, righteousness, and justice with His mercy and love. Now God can offer you forgiveness if you repent (turn from your sin) and have faith in the One who paid this debt for you. The apostle Paul wrote, "Therefore being justified by faith we have peace (our debt is paid) with God" (Romans 5:1). Hallelujah! Your sin can be forgiven. Our debt is paid!

Students, I drew up this diagram to give you a picture of this potential dilemma that God faced for you to keep in your Bible Studies notebooks. I will be looking for them there when I grade them.

Closing Prayer:

Oh God, from all eternity You had a plan to redeem Your people. We stand in awe at Your wisdom and the sacrifice You made to rescue us from ourselves by paying the debt we owed to You. We will be forever grateful and thankful to You for sending Christ to rescue us, and our thankfulness will go on for all eternity. Amen.

Truth Theme: The Atonement = Our debt is paid.

coach@chapelfield.org

CHAPEL TALK
38
Why Coldenham?

"[A]nd there shall be famines, and pestilences, and earthquakes, in divers places. All these are the beginning of sorrows."

Matthew 24:7-8

WHY COLDENHAM?

Background: On November 16, 1989, a brick wall at Coldenham Elementary School, a school in our community, came crashing down during a very violent, freak wind storm, killing nine children. Our community was devastated. I only had a few minutes to speak to our students about it because we were rushed that morning.

Kids, the National Aviation and Transportation Safety Board gave the following probable cause for the tragedy when a 727 plummeted into the Potomac River on snowy December afternoon, killing seventy-eight passengers: "Human error and the forces of nature." From almost the beginning of time, man has had to battle his own failures and a hostile environment. Why is this? Man was not created to err, and nature was not created to harass. However, the Bible makes it clear that when man decided he knew more than God, his environment became his antagonist and he was forced to live with his limitations— his errors. God did not cause man to go against His laws or to violate God's requirements every day. The question is not, "Why Coldenham?" The question is, "Why not me?" Why does He allow any of us to live at all? The answer is found in His mercy. He is merciful, allowing us time and opportunity to turn in humility, in confession, and acceptance of His salvation in Christ before the final catastrophe when all opportunity will be gone. Coldenham was not an act of God, nor an act of nature.

The tragedy of Coldenham was caused by the inability of human beings (limited beings) to cope with our own sinful natures and our hostile environments. Both failed their original purposes. No matter how sophisticated we become, we will build walls that will fall, planes that will crash. Kids, no matter how well we protect ourselves, earthquakes will devastate us, hurricanes will ravage us, and disease will conquer us. For the children of Coldenham, they are in the care of a just and loving God. For those of us who remain, the Bible gives two astonishing promises. Soon, it says, nature will no longer be hostile for "the wolf will lie down with the lamb" (Isaiah 11:6) and soon there will be no more human error! All believers shall come "unto the perfect man" (Ephesians 4:13). What a great day! No more walls constructed by humans that will crash down! No more tragedy!

Yet the qualification of Jesus thunders from the crumbled walls of the Tower of Siloam that killed eighteen when it fell: "Nay: but except ye repent, ye shall all likewise perish!" (Luke 13:5).

Kids, I may have rushed this morning but as you leave, make sure you rush away with the moral of Coldenham—life is very unpredictable; make sure in your heart that you are ready to meet the God that requires you to repent so that you may have ultimate safety and peace.

Closing Prayer:

Oh Lord Jesus, through the clamor and tragedies of nature's violent fury, help us find safety in You. We pray for the families that lost their children at Coldenham. Oh God, their pain is incomprehensible. Comfort them right now with the knowledge that their children are in the hands of a just and loving God. In Jesus's name, we ask this. Amen.

Truth Theme: In this life, great tragedies will always be around us, and some will affect us personally. The only hope for us is the loving arms of Jesus.

coach@chapelfield.org

CHAPEL TALK
39

"Crazy Lou" Taught Me How to Worship

"Our worship produces a desire in us to produce worship in others."

Author, in his book,
"The Obstacle Course"

A Thought for Today

"CRAZY LOU" TAUGHT ME
HOW TO WORSHIP!

Kids, let's use the early church as our example of how to worship God and Christ. The early Christians came together mainly to pray, to hear from a knowledgeable biblical speaker (now called a preacher), to take the sacrament of communion, sing hymns (mainly the Psalms) and bring others–believers and non-believers alike–with them, thus providing fellowship and support with other Christians and this was called worship.

Now look at our church services today. Although many have these essential ingredients of the early church meetings, many have added entertainment, supposed healings, seeker-friendly devices, movies, and high-tech electronic displays, as well as extra-biblical messages such as positive thinking, prosperity guarantees, exotic speaking and liberal theology to their forms of worship.

Some people say that I am old-fashioned, but I like the early church model. It centered on prayer, exhortation, communion, singing and praising, bringing others to Christ as well as sometimes taking up a collection to help the poor or support missionaries. That is all. No Hollywood attractions, no sensational practices, or Park Avenue slick talkers to draw people in. Moreover, no soft theology designed to please the listener—just static and conductive worship. By static, I mean worship that raises praise and thankfulness up to God. By conductive, I mean outreach to the local and greater community that accomplishes the mission of Christ by meeting human need and preaching the gospel. That is true worship. It is both static, emanating up to God vertically and conductive, horizontal, accomplishing something, namely the commands of our Lord in Matthew 25:31-46—meeting human need, and Matthew 28:19-20—going into all the world and preaching the gospel.

So kids, my advice to you is to find a church that, first of all, has good Reformation teaching and also has both static and conductive worship. I want to tell you a brief story. When I was a young college student working over the summer to get money for my next year's studies, I got a job as a carpenter's helper. My boss, Lou Vanderplate, was thought to be a crazy guy by most of my Christian friends. He had bought a dilapidated old church down the road and had me and his carpenter work fixing it up. What a job! The roof was leaking, and the doors would not open. And then he bought an old school bus. I thought to myself, "Why the heck does he want this old wreck?"

"Bill," he said to me, "Every Sunday morning I want you to drive it to three pre-set locations in nearby town. Pull the bus over at these stops, open the door, wait ten minutes, and then go to the next stop. Do the same at the next two stops and then come back to our church."

School bus

I looked at him like he was crazy. No one was going to just climb on to a bus that shows up unexpectedly on a Sunday morning. In the meantime, Lou had stuck two big banners on the sides of the bus announcing, "Church bus pick up at 9:30. Drop off after coffee hour at 12:30." He was my boss, so I did as he asked. For three consecutive Sundays, I waited on the bus and returned alone to the church where I sat with the carpenter and his family for morning worship. I wasn't sure how Lou felt, but I was feeling a bit discouraged. And then, on the fourth Sunday, I was amazed when two women and a child were waiting at the stop and climbed on. For the first time, I pulled up to the church with passengers! I felt like I had a purpose. The next Sunday four or five more people got on, and soon I was carrying a full bus with a couple of passengers standing. I began to think that Lou was far from crazy. Lou's worship service was both static and conductive.

Summer was ending, and I had to go back to college, and my carpenter friend, John, took over the run. Many years later when Kathy and I were married, we attended a little church which had a dedicated and friendly congregation and a fine preacher. But sadly, half of the seats on Sunday mornings were empty. Knowing that there was a large, poor, mostly minority community just a couple of miles away, and having a large school bus that was not used on Sunday mornings, I thought back to Lou's bus run and approached a couple of the elders in the church with my Vanderplate idea. But to my surprise, one elder said that this did not fit the style of that church's ministry, and the other merely smiled and said nothing. Realizing this was a new concept for this body, I waited and tried again another time. But the result was the same. Not wanting to be divisive, I resisted the urge to try again. I settled for my church being great in static worship, but not willing to engage in conductive practice at all—resisting even the consideration of such a change. It was not complete worship.

Kids, I tell you this story because you and your future family (especially your children) will need to see and experience a church that is worshiping in "spirit and in truth"—one whose worship is both static and conductive. I pray that you will seek that also.

Closing Prayer:

Oh, our Father, who is all worthy of our most and truly meaningful worship. Teach us how to look beyond worship that falsely satisfies our shallow expectation of what worship is and replace it with true worship that emanates up to You and reaches out in love in our neighbors in this lost world. Amen

Truth Theme: A true Christian will have the desire to pray, listen and sing, as well as go, share, and love. Don't settle for anything less in worship.

coach@chapelfield.org

CHAPEL TALK
40
Why Did You Have to Kick So Many Out?

"And they laughed him to scorn. But [Jesus] put them all out."

Mark 5:40

WHY DID YOU HAVE TO KICK SO MANY OUT?

Principal kicking student out

<u>Background</u>: I recently heard a sermon by Rev. Carlton Byrd on Mark 5:21-43 that reminded me of a similar situation I had in 1995. At that time, I had to ask fifteen students to transfer to other schools. This was about half of our student body at the time. It really hurt us financially. Here's the reason why.

Kids, many of you know I had to ask fifteen boys to leave the school. I think most of you know the reason why I had to do this. I will briefly go over these reasons with you this morning, but there's one reason for doing this that I feel is most important.

When your parents came in to register you at Chapel Field, I carefully explained to them that we here are a standards-based school, not a compassion-based school, like some others in our area. By that I meant that if your parents wanted discipline, structure, and a vision for future accomplishments, we are the right place to come; if you want compassion after they seriously screw up or repeatedly screw up after a second chance, then go to church and be counseled by a pastor. That is a pastor's job. The sign outside our school does not say "Chapel Field Church" or "Day Care Center;" it says "School," a place of learning and of serious education. This formally rules out a play place or a reform school. That does not mean kids, that we won't have fun, joke around with you, play sports, and rejoice in victories with you. But it does mean, however, that we are serious about providing you with the knowledge, character, and intelligence you will need to face your future in an evil world with confidence and the ability to represent your Lord and be successful in your futures.

So, having listened to what I have said, here are four reasons I had to ask these kids to leave. I want to give you the three "fors" of Christian education. The first "for" is understanding, knowledge, and wisdom. That's all that Christian education is trying to do for you! Solomon wrote, "The heart of him that hath understanding seeketh knowledge," (Proverbs 15:14) and "In the lips of him that hath understanding wisdom is found" (Proverbs 10:13). Note students, that he says "seeketh." Jesus said, "Ask, and it shall be given you; seek, and ye shall find; knock, and it shall be opened unto you" (Matthew 7:7). Why did He say that? Because seeking and knocking require effort, dedication to finding answers, results.

Again, from observing these boys and their casual attitude and behavior for several months, it was obvious they did not want this for themselves and because of the distraction they caused, they did not want it for you either. I reminded them over and over, counseled with them and their parents. I reminded them that this is a school dedicated to teaching them these three important truths, not a playground for fun only, but they would not adjust their behavior. So, I let them go. I thought I might be saving their parents a lot of grief and money.

The second "for" is character. Kids, character is developed by understanding the truth. That's what will set you free in life. Jesus went on to say, "I am the truth." So, we want to know all about Jesus (that's why we have an intense Biblical Studies program here). For Jesus, truth and character are one.

I was once counseling a boy because he was viewing inappropriate things on his cell phone and showing them to others at home. I told him that he could not do this because our honor code says that proper behavior is required in and out of school. He responded, "What I do at home is my business!" I said, "Your business equals your reputation. Your reputation will be your character. Once that is ruined by immorality or lying about it, you will have a very hard time earning people's trust again, if ever."

And finally, on this character issue, you have often heard me refer to the Rotten Apple Theory, where rotten apples will spoil all the good apples in the basket. Kids, I can't let rotten apples here affect your search for understanding, knowledge, wisdom, and the truth. Your character depends on it.

Thirdly, vision. Solomon reminds us, "without vision the people perish" (Proverbs 20:18). I asked most of these boys what their vision was for their future. In other words, what did they want to do with their lives? What was next for their education?

"I don't know," most answered. What? No hope or plans for the future? No vision? If they don't get it, they will perish. I did not want these apples to turn you rotten also. I once had a ruckus in class when the teacher stepped out for a moment. It got really bad. Things were broken. So, I asked a girl, who was of model character, who was responsible. Now I had a policy that I would never give an informant's name. I would just say, "I heard that you did this," and wait for the answer. But this good, honest girl, she lied to me! And others did likewise. Right there I knew I had to get rid of these apples. They affect even the best apples.

The final "for" is for miracles still to happen. My teachers and I had a vision of what this school could do and be. We had already seen four or five divine interventions in the way this little school began (see my book, *The Obstacle Course* for the stories related to these interventions). We wanted these to continue. In Mark 5:21-43, Jesus wanted to do a miracle to heal a little girl but the people all around Jesus "laughed at him and mocked him" (verse 40). Then Jesus had to kick them all out (verse 40) in order to do the miracle. Those with no vision and little character had to go. Kids, if you want God to do great things in your life now and in the future, doubters, scoffers, negative people, and bad apples will have to go. Make sure you are on the right side of the "but." I remember vividly what my missions professor told me in college in 1961. "Make sure you are always on the right side of the 'but.'" You may have bad influences around you. Don't say, "I have the Lord but all these bad influences." Say, "I have all these bad influences, but I have the Lord."

Remember kids, Jesus is still our miracle-worker. Refuse to be around anybody that will interfere with your vision of what the Lord has for you—get them out! Get understanding, knowledge, wisdom, character, and vision. Pray and miracles will happen in your life.

Closing Prayer:

Oh Lord, make us realize the truth of what our education should be. Help us to avoid, at all costs, bad influences attacking our lives. We pray for those that had to leave us. Help them to discover these principles of our learning that You have carefully laid out for us in Your Word, that they might have the vision and character for You to work miracles for them also. We ask this in Jesus's name. Amen.

Truth Theme: Get bad influences out of your life and be on the right side of the "but."

coach@chapelfield.org

CHAPEL TALK
41
Hast Thou Considered My Servant Job?

"Do not be proud, boasting to others,
but have pride in your God and your
Holy-Spirit-guided faithfulness to Him."

Author

A Thought for Today:

HAST THOU CONSIDERED MY SERVANT JOB?

Background: We had a robust discussion in class regarding the subject of pride, so I decided to do a chapel on it.

Kids, regarding the three major sins listed in 1 John 2:16 (the lust of the flesh, the lust of the eyes, and the pride of life), what is pride? Webster says, on one hand, pride is self-respect. On the other, it says that it is conceit or arrogance. Why are there two kinds of pride, and if there are, which kind is good, and which is bad? We must make a distinction between good pride and bad pride.

A better definition of good pride is when you have joy in your own and other's successes or accomplishments. For example, your parents may say that they're proud of your good grades in school. You may be proud that you did that also. People take pride in their sports teams, their heroes, their schools, their diplomas, or degrees. This kind of pride builds up your confidence and leads to success in life. This pride is a good thing.

However, when we say a person is prideful (full of pride), that's another thing altogether. This kind of pride departs from good pride in that it seeks to be boosted and superior over others. How many times have you heard on the playground, "I am better than you are."? These kinds of kids, when they grow up, are like the boxer Muhammed Ali, who said of himself, "I am the great one." Prideful people always want to belittle you and make you feel inferior. This kind of pride "goes before the fall." Lance Armstrong comes to mind. It is said that he boasted that no one else would be able to win three Tour de France races in a row. Well, hello, Lance. Your three trophies were taken away for doping, and your fall was great.

God also has pride. He is proud of you when you seek to walk after Him. "And the LORD said unto Satan, 'Hast thou considered my servant Job, that there is none like him in the earth, a perfect and an upright man, one that feareth God, and escheweth evil?'" (Job 1:8). God, the Holy One of Israel, the creator of the universe, the Savior of His people through the sacrifice of His Son Jesus, is proud of you! Don't let a prideful, superior, boastful heart destroy the pride that a loving God has for you. Put your name in the last word of this sentence, "Satan, hast thou considered My servant (your name)? He/She fears Me and abhors evil."

God proud of His servant, Job

Closing Prayer:

Oh Lord, keep us from prideful hearts that destroy others. Inspire us toward accomplishments and successes in Your service. We are proud that You are our creator, our God, and our Savior, through our Lord, Jesus Christ. Amen.

Truth Theme: Be proud that God has given you rebirth by the power of His Holy Spirit. Now make Him proud of you by striving to demonstrate character and righteousness that will glorify Him.

coach@chapelfield.org

CHAPEL TALK
42
Are You Loved Unconditionally?

"If you want to experience the love of God
in Jesus Christ, you will have to meet
His necessary conditions."

R.C. Sproul

A Thought for Today

ARE YOU LOVED UNCONDITIONALLY?

<u>Background</u>: A class discussion provoked controversy over whether God places conditions on His love for mankind. So, I decided to do a chapel on the subject.

Kids, I am going to use an expletive in chapel today; out of the biblical context, it is an inappropriate word. However, I am going to use it to make a major theological point; so please don't go home to your parents tonight and say, "Coach swore in chapel today." I'll get all kinds of phone calls and emails tomorrow!

In our Christian culture today, we are obsessed with the idea of God's grandfatherly love the He lavishes upon all mankind "unconditionally." How many times have you heard, "God loves you unconditionally," or "God is love," or seen bumper stickers, "God loves you?"

I had a dream one night that I was driving behind a car driven by Mike Tyson. Tyson was, at one time, the heavyweight champion of the world. He was very stocky and muscular and very intimidating. On his rear bumper there was a sticker that read, "I am mad as hell at Coach Spanjer, and when I see him, I am going to knock his block off!" (I had to tailgate him to read the words, but I did.)

In my dream, I went straight home, called Mike up and asked him why he was so angry with me. "Coach," he said, "you have slandered my name and used it in curse words. I heard that you mocked the rules I live by and lusted after my daughter. Further, I noticed that you have been coveting my money and my success."

I said, "Mike, I know I have done these things and cursed your name. I sincerely apologize and am very sorry—please forgive me. I won't do those things again."

Mike answered, "I accept your apology and your sorrow for having said these nasty things. I am okay with you now."

I ask you, which bumper sticker drove me to repentance? One that said, "I love Coach Spanjer" or the sticker that said, "I am mad as hell at Coach"? Of course, the "mad as hell" sticker drove me to confess my sin toward Mike. An "I love you" sticker would just make me feel good and would continue to go about my regular violations of Mike's character.

Kids, the apostle Paul says that we were enemies of God (Romans 5:10). Why does the apostle Paul say that about us? Because we violate His laws, slander His name and His character every day! Since we are created in God's image, required to reflect His character at all times, when we lie, lust, envy, and gossip, we say God is like this also! If someone said all these things about you, would you be happy with them? I think not!

Bumper stickers that say God loves you are self-defeating, misrepresenting the truth. Of course, the love of God is unconditional for all mankind under His common grace. All men get life, sunshine, and rain to survive. But to get past final judgment and eternal damnation, there are necessary conditions you and I must meet. Just like I did to Mike Tyson, I had to admit my sins against him (confess) and say truthfully that I am sorry (repent)—necessary conditions to have right standing with Mike.

The Bible holds up eternal life to us, but it is conditional upon repentance—"Nay, except ye repent" there is no salvation (Luke 13:3, 5). And faith in Jesus Christ, "If you confess with your mouth Jesus as Lord and believe in your heart that God raised Him from the dead, thou shalt be saved" (Romans 10: 9,

10). Don't believe those who say God loves you unconditionally.

What are you going to do with Him? Believe and trust in Him or be condemned forever? The apostle John says in 1 John 4:8 "God is love." A familiar text. However, people don't read what follows—"This was manifest (made clear) because God sent His only son into the world that we might live through Him." The saving love is only revealed in Jesus Christ. Why? Because He died to pay our debt to God, for profaning His character. He died receiving our punishment so we can receive His life! That is the gospel.

So, wrapping that up—all men enjoy God's love under common grace, but only those who repent and trust Christ enjoy God's saving love under special grace.

Now I am not going to get a bumper sticker on my truck that says, "God is mad as hell at you." What doctor, when he discovers you have cancer says, "I love you. Go home you'll be okay."? No, he recommends surgery or whatever treatment will help you. The world wants a God that says, "I love you; go home. You'll be okay," when actually the disease will be killing them all for eternity. The cure, kids, is the gospel. Christ cured you (paid your debt) on the cross, but it will only be effective if you repent and have faith in Him alone. Have you met His conditions?

Closing Prayer:

Oh, God, help us to recognize the truth and avoid those who tell us falsehoods and lead us down the broad road to destruction. We pray that Your Holy Spirit will cause us to meet Your conditions of faith and repentance in Jesus Christ alone that we may have peace and live with You for all eternity. Amen

Truth Theme: All humanity experiences God's love every day through all the joys of living. However, God's greater saving love rescuing us from death and hell comes to us only when we meet His condition of faith and repentance in Jesus Christ alone. Don't let anyone tell you otherwise.

coach@chapelfield.org

CHAPEL TALK
43

"Hey, Coach! Can My Prayers Really Be Answered?"

"If the veil of the world's machinery were lifted off, how much we would find is done in answer to the prayers of God's children?"

Robert Murray McCheyne

A Thought for Today

HEY COACH! CAN MY PRAYERS REALLY BE ANSWERED?

<u>Background</u>: This question is common with teens struggling with the question: God seems so far away; can He really answer my prayers? So, I answered it this way:

Kids, this question comes from a complete misunderstanding of who God is. The theologians speak of God's holiness as being transcendent (far) and His power being immanent (close). Let me explain. All of you point to where you think God is. [The students all pointed up.] You are only partially right, but that partial answer gives us a wrong impression of God. God is not far in distance but is far in degree, a totally different dimension, a sphere that we just cannot see into. Our human perception (senses) are limited to the material world. The Bible tells us that God is omnipresent—everywhere at one time. The psalmist wrote in Psalm 139:

> *Whither shall I go from Your Spirit, or whither shall I flee from Your presence? If I ascend up to heaven Thou are there. If I make my bed in hell behold Thou are there. If I take the wings of the morning and swell in the outermost parts of the sea, even there shall Thy hand lead me, and Thy right hand shall hold me.*

How can we say God is far then? Because that dimension for us might as well be as far as the east is from the west. We can neither see it nor comprehend this concept. However, the Bible says that God is nearer to us than a brother (as close as our genes are—that's near!) and sees us at every moment, when we are doing good things or bad things. There are no private moments for us that God does not see. That's scary! Although we cannot see into that world, God gave us a glimpse into it in 2 Kings 6. In this text, Elisha's city was surrounded by the King of Syria's army. Elisha's servant began to panic. Then God allowed the servant to see into God's dimension, and "behold, the mountains were full of horses and chariots of fire around Elisha." Kids, that's what's possible in that dimension around us.

This is the centuries-old dispute whether God is totally transcendent, far. But, we said earlier that God, though transcendent (far) as our senses are concerned, He is also immanent (near) to us in His power. That's why our prayers can be answered, and we get guidance. It's the same power that is seen in Christ's incarnation, His miracles, His atonement, and resurrection. So, that's why we say God is both far and near at the same time.

But kids, let me warn you, you will be going out into a "Christian" world where many ministers and people believe that God is only far, that miracles can't happen, that the resurrection can't happen and that you and I can't be born again. These people are called deists, liberals, or nowadays, neo-modernists. But we here at Chapel Field, as in most of your churches believe, yes, God is far in His holiness, majesty, and purity but very near to us in His power to save us, answer our prayers and guide us to victory and eternal life.

This truth is clearly seen in the inspired story of Jacob's ladder. You remember that episode found in Genesis 28:10-17. What he saw there proved both the deist and liberal wrong, if you believe the word of God. Jacob, running for his life from his brother Esau, stopped at a place somewhere between Beersheba and Padan-Aram to rest for the night. There Jacob fell asleep and had a vision that changed his life forever. He saw a ladder going from him to heaven far above him. On the top was God and Jacob was at the bottom. Angels were going up and down the ladder, up to God (far) and down to Jacob (near). God told Jacob these words: "I am with thee, and will keep thee in all places whither thou goest," (verse 15). Now remember Jesus's words in Matthew 28:20, "I am with you always, even unto the end of the world."

So, kids, God may be far in His holiness and purity, so we are protected from His wrath, for we are sinners, but He is close to us in His power to protect us from the evil one. You can depend upon it—Christ, being God, is with us and will answer your prayers. "If you ask anything in My name" (for His purposes) "I will do it." This is how this school is here. He will do it for you.

Closing Prayer:

Oh God, please shield us from the terrors of those who deny Your transcendence or Your immanence. We know that You are far in order to save us from Your holiness destroying us now but close in Christ to save us from Your judgment. Amen.

Truth Theme: If you ever have doubt as to where God is, remember Jacob's ladder. If you are escaping from this world to His purposes, He will be with you. You can count on it!

coach@chapelfield.org

CHAPEL TALK
44
"What's the Big Deal with My Friends?"

"He that walketh with wise men shall be wise:
but a companion of fools shall be destroyed."

Proverbs 13:20

A Thought for Today

WHAT'S THE BIG DEAL WITH MY FRIENDS?

<u>Background</u>: Over the years as principal, I've had many complaints from parents, "I don't like the friends my son (or daughter) hangs out with." From *students,* I'd hear, "My parents complain about my friends. What's their problem?" So, I decided to do a thought for today to address this issue.

Kids, several years ago, I had identical twins in school, Janine and Jennifer. Since I had them for only one class a day, it took me several months to figure out who was who. During that time, I would often address one, "Janine, study harder next time," and more often than not, the reply would come back, "I'm not Janine; I'm Jennifer." One day I overheard Jennifer joke, "Hey Janine, you're getting me in trouble." Jennifer had every right to complain. Janine was a visible copy of her sister. If one goofed off, or vice versa, it reflected on the other also.

So it is with you and me and God. We are copies of God, in the moral and ethical sense. The Bible says that we are created in His own image. When we claim to be Christians and identify with those who are immoral in their lifestyles or actions, whether they are rock stars or classmates, we make God's image look bad! That is no small matter. It is a strike at God's holiness and purity—a sin, the Bible tells us that borders on the unpardonable. In Romans 1:23-26, the apostle Paul said, mankind, changed the glory of the incorruptible God for the likeness of the image of corruptible man. Therefore God gave them up in the lusts of their hearts. For they exchanged the truth of God for a lie.

Kids, this reminds us that when we poorly reflect or change God's image to an impure one, we lie and run the risk of being given up by God.

Gang of teens

Your parents have good reason to be concerned about your friends, your appearance, and your activities. They love you very much and want you to have the best reputation possible. Just as a mirror always reflects the image in front of it, everything we do reflects either positively or negatively on God. There is no middle ground. Jesus said, "He who is not with me is against me" (Matthew 12:30).

Isn't it great that purity, modesty, and wholesome friends identify us positively with the creator of the universe? You are at a point of conflict. God is testing you. As a copy of Him, you have the tremendous opportunity to reflect His image rightly. Take advantage of it. Your identity will not be mistaken.

Closing Prayer:

Oh God, please forgive us when we identify with those that misrepresent You. Please guide us to genuine friends with good Christian character so that all of us will be pleasing in Your sight. Amen.

Truth Theme: Your reputation will mainly depend on who your friends are. Remember who your "twin" is.

coach@chapelfield.org

45

Will the Real God Please Stand Up?

"Thou didst hide Thy face and I was troubled"—but—"The heavens declare the glory of God and the firmament showeth forth His handiwork."

Psalm 30:10; 19:1

A Thought for Today

WILL THE REAL GOD PLEASE STAND UP?

Background: This question has haunted many a Christian. If God is real, why doesn't He just show Himself to us? If He did, we would believe! This proposition came up in *class* and having a brief time in *chapel* that day, I decided to handle it like this.

Kids, the question was asked: if God is real, why doesn't He just reveal Himself and then we would believe. Jesus Himself handled this question. In His lifetime when He told this parable: A rich man died and went to hell. In that place of torment, he cried out to Abraham in heaven "Please send Lazarus to tell my father and brothers to repent and avoid this terrible place." Abraham replied, "Even if they see Lazarus raised from the dead, they will not believe. Let them heed Moses and the prophets." (story in Matthew 16:19-31).

In other words, kids, such a visitation would not help you to believe or repent. Instead, we must have faith in the word of God. Faith will give us the real light to see. To fully understand, we must consider three truths. First, God's reality is visible, and we know it. When we look at the stars and the intricacies of the human body and indeed of all creation, we see the workmanship of God, and we all know He exists. Second, the Bible tells us that the greatest favor God did for man was to not let us see the fullness of His presence. If He came into our room, we would disintegrate in a flash! "No man can see God and live," says the Bible in Exodus 33:20. Our sinfulness and selfishness could not stand the impact of the holiness, purity, and righteousness of our God. Thus, God's physical absence is

Chapel Time **With Teens - For Parents**

a blessing which provides us time to understand how we can one day enter His presence. Third, at one time God did become physically visible in the person of His Son. As Jesus affirmed, "If you have seen Me, you have seen the Father." As God could call nature into being by the sound of His voice, Jesus could control nature by the sound of His voice. Storms were stopped, the blind could see, the lame could walk, and, with the holy power of God, the dead came back to life. The problem was that God was not safe in the hands of His creatures—we killed Him! I have often wondered why He chose to visit us at all, but He did and overcame death also. Isn't it wonderful that He now says that simple things like faith, belief, and repentance will one day usher us into His presence forever? When you think about it, faith is the perfect way.

Closing Prayer:

Our Heavenly Father, please take away our blindness and let us see, by faith, Your presence, by faith, Your Son and, by faith, Your Salvation in Him. Amen.

Truth Theme: We have all the evidence necessary to believe— the evidence of His creation and the evidence of His presence in Jesus of Nazareth. We are without excuse.

coach@chapelfield.org

CHAPEL TALK

46

Are Catholics Christians?

"*Peace (with God) is not to be had
by the sacrifice of the truth*"

John Calvin,
Tracts and Traces of John Calvin.

A Thought for Today

ARE CATHOLICS CHRISTIANS?

<u>Background:</u> This question came up in class in various forms over the years. The question was, why the Catholic students called themselves "Roman Catholics" and the Protestant students just called themselves Christians. So, our Catholic students wondered why. Here was my brief answer:

Students, and particularly to my Catholic students, I want to say this: Anybody who professes Jesus Christ is God, truly repents and believes in His resurrection, has faith in Him alone, and seeks to live a Christian life of obedience to Him is a Christian, regardless of what church he or she attends. Notice I said in Christ alone, not in an institution. An institution cannot save you, no matter how many steps they have or what sacraments they demand, no matter what their theology is or what their leaders say. Only your personal relationship with Jesus Christ counts. The reason I say this is because most Catholics I know believe in Jesus but count on the Roman religion equally to get them into heaven, not Jesus Christ **alone**. The church, for true Christians, is a place to worship God, partake of the sacraments (baptism and communion) and fellowship with other Christians. It is not to be **trusted in**. Most Catholics trust in the institution and Jesus Christ equally and not in Christ alone.

Kids, I stopped calling Roman Catholicism a church long ago. I refer to it as the Roman religion. Here's why. There are eight essentials necessary to be a true Christian church. They are beliefs in:

1. The Incarnation–this includes the virgin birth and the deity of Jesus Christ
2. The gospel–Jesus Christ's message that salvation is by God's grace and through faith alone
3. The Sacraments–baptism, communion, and the worship of God's people (reading of scripture, singing of hymns, praise, prayer, and evangelism—inviting others to these services and to believe in Jesus Christ)
4. The Atonement–the debt we owe to God being paid by Christ's propitiation
5. The Resurrection–Christ being raised from the dead bodily
6. The Ascension–Christ's exaltation to God's right hand to rule over His kingdom
7. The Second Coming of Christ–Christ's return to judge mankind and extend rewards and inheritance to His people ushering them into the new world.
8. The Holy Scriptures–the sole and final authority for faith and practice

Kids, since the Roman religion does not believe in two of these essentials, I can't call it a church. First, it denies the gospel of salvation by grace and faith alone. The Roman religion teaches that salvation is by works and merits to finally earn your salvation and right standing with God. Secondly, they do not believe that the scriptures are the sole and final authority for faith and practice for God's people. The Roman religion has four authorities:

1. The pope (he is their final authority)

2. The councils and creeds

3. Their traditions

4. The Bible

So, when a vote is taken on any particular doctrine, and it's 3-to-1 against the Bible, if it goes against the pope's wishes, he has veto power. What's more, kids, the Catholics add to the sacraments at least four more extra-biblical sacraments, plus they promote transubstantiation as part of the communion service (this is the belief that Jesus's body is physically present in the communion and He is crucified over and over again at each mass).

And lastly, the Roman Catholic religion also has two heresies that are not in Holy Scriptures at all. First is the worship of Mary and the saints. The Bible calls this idolatry—"You shall [worship] no other gods beside Me" (Exodus 20:3, AMP). The apostle Paul wrote, "They worshiped and served what was created rather than the creator" (Romans 1:25). Further, "Make no graven images" (Exodus 20:4). Second is the doctrine of purgatory, which is nowhere in the Bible. This dreadful, horrid place of punishment awaits every Catholic. No Roman Catholic has true peace with God. But the Bible says, "Therefore being justified by faith we have **peace** with God through our Lord Jesus Christ" (Romans 5:1).

Souls suffering in Purgatory

So, this is why I cannot call Roman Catholicism a church. And you should not either. However, anyone that trusts in the finished work of Christ alone for their right standing with God (salvation) and not an institution are true Christians. And many Catholics do and are. However, they have a lot of false teachings to endure, which I know from experience (you can read about my personal exit from Catholicism in my book *The Obstacle Course*). I hope that this answers your questions and encourages you to always seek truth over and above an institution.

Closing Prayer:

Oh, Father, You ask each of us to come to You in faith and believe in Your son Jesus Christ. Nothing in our hands we bring—no merit, no works, no faith in any other things. Thank You for welcoming us with open and loving arms, this by Your grace and mercy alone. Amen.

Truth Theme: You are a Christian by God's grace and through your faith in His Son alone. Thus, you are a member of the church of the Lord Jesus Christ.

coach@chapelfield.org

CHAPEL TALK
47
Our American Flag– Will You Honor It?

"Oh beautiful, for heroes proved, in liberating strife, who more than self, their country loved, and mercy more than life. America, America, God shed His grace on thee."

"America the Beautiful,"
Katherine Lee Bates

OUR AMERICAN FLAG—
WILL YOU HONOR IT?

Kids, why do we have three flagpoles on our campus? I will have more when our new athletic fields are complete. Why? I was a boy of six when World War II started. I rode my bike up and down the streets of our small town and saw the stars in almost every window, representing sons that went to fight in that war. I still remember in my mind the wailing and crying of the mothers of my neighbors when the chaplain would come down the walks of their homes with the announcement that their son was killed in action." Kids, that left a big and very lasting impression on me, even to this day.

Flag waving

Over 250,000 mothers' sons never came home from that war. Why? Because they died honoring and defending our flag. These boys would never have families, have children, go to Little League games with their kids. They gave up their right to have girlfriends, wives, Christmas holidays and family reunions. Why did they go? What were they willing to lay their lives down the for? I know, because of family values, our freedoms of religion and free speech, for the rights for others to have the potential to prosper, and traditional family values. They died to protect free enterprise, our Constitution, moral democracy. They died for Americanism! This, so that you and I could do all these things.

I can't honor them by going to all their gravesites or offering a hug to their moms. The only way I can honor them is saying the Pledge of Allegiance and by honoring the flag that draped their coffins when their bodies were shipped back home. We must live out the virtues they made the ultimate sacrifice for.

In our country today, there is tremendous disrespect for our leaders, our institutions and our national symbols. Cartoonists and comedians go beyond the limits of good taste, protestors show arrogant disrespect. And religious groups do not honor our flag because they say that they answer to a higher authority. However, all these people are in direct opposition to the Bible. The Bible commands respect and honor be given to our government, its representatives and thus, its symbols. Jesus said to honor Caesar by paying his taxes; the apostle Paul said, "Give respect to whom respect is due and honor to who honor is due" (Romans 13:7).

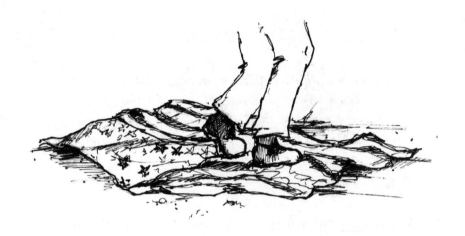

People desecrating the American flag

Those who disrespect our flag, whether individuals, groups, or companies, are not true Americans. They're just squatters here, enjoying what others died to provide for them. Kids, they deserve to live under a socialist and poverty-stricken dictatorship. Then they might appreciate our flag! Honor is due to a president who takes his oath upon the Bible. Honor is due to the dead that gave their lives protecting us. And honor is due to the American flag.

It always seemed strange to me that certain people and groups dishonor the very country that protects them and their rights. Just as there is no greater virtue than to do good to those who hate you, there is no greater evil than to slap the face of someone (or in this case, a country) who has helped you. Whether a law is passed to protect our flag or not, citizens who disrespect the flag or ignore it will answer to that Higher Authority.

Closing Prayer:

Heavenly Father, You have given us the privilege to be born in the greatest country in the world, founded mostly by men who trusted in You. What a great legacy of heroes we have. Bless our fallen and bless our flag. Amen.

Truth Theme: There is no greater love than this, that one lays down his life for his friend. And no greater honor can be given to those who did than to honor the flag that they died for.

coach@chapelfield.org

CHAPEL TALK

48

Was God Joking with Adam and Eve?

"[F]or in the day that thou eatest thereof thou shalt surely die."

Genesis 2:17

A Thought for Today

WAS GOD JOKING WITH ADAM AND EVE?

Background: A student raised this question in class: was God joking with Adam and Eve when He said, "The day you eat, you will surely die" (Genesis 2:16)? They didn't die; so, was God joking around with them? Knowing I only had a short time this particular morning, I gave a brief chapel on the subject.

Good morning, kids. Given that we only have a short time this morning, I would like to answer the question Brian brought up in class yesterday. Was God joking when He told Adam and Eve, "The day you eat of the Tree of the Knowledge of Good and Evil, you will surely die"? They did not die that day. Was God joking with them?

God was not joking. Some people try to explain this apparent discrepancy by saying that Adam and Eve died spiritually; that is, they died in the sense that they lost fellowship with God. This explanation, however, does not do justice to the text. The Bible says, "The day you eat, you will die."

Adam and Eve in the garden

The answer lies in the wonderful, loving mercy of God. When Adam and Eve disobeyed, God did what every executive—though not required to do—has the right to do. He did not give justice, which would have meant immediate death, but He gave mercy in the form of executive clemency. He allowed a stay, or reprieve, in executing His judgment. In theology, this stay or reprieve, is called *common grace*, which means free life to all men for a period of time. We all have a life sentence—we will all die.

But the good news is that we all have a lifetime, however long or short, to turn from our own disobedience to God's law and, by faith, trust the One who kept it perfectly and thus be reunited eternally with our God.

Ronald Monroe, once an inmate on death row, had been convicted of brutally murdering his landlady, mother of two, Lenora Collins in 1977. Louisiana Governor, Charles Roemer, granted Monroe a stay of execution, buying time for more facts and evidence to be brought forth in the case. According to the Bible, all of humanity is on death row. The only fact that will save us is whether we have trusted the substitute God sent to die in our place, satisfying His just wrath. If this is true, those who believe will pass from death to life eternal and avoid the consequences of the day when our stay of execution is revoked.

Closing Prayer:

Oh God, forgive the day we take Your words as a joke. Clear our minds. What You say will happen. While our stay is being granted, help us to trust the Substitute You sent to take our penalty, Jesus Christ, thereby revoking our death sentence and granting us eternal life. Amen.

Truth Theme: The evidence is in, and judgment has been passed; we will die. Some will pass into eternal death and others will pass into eternal life—the choice is ours.

coach@chapelfield.org

CHAPEL TALK
49
Who Is Your God?
(Part I)

> "What were we made for? To know God. What aim should we have in life? To know God. What is the eternal life that Jesus gives? To know God. What is the best thing in life? To know God. What in humans gives God most pleasure? Knowledge of himself."
>
> J. I. Packer

A Thought for Today

WHO IS YOUR GOD?
(Part I)

Background: I did these theological chapel talks every once in a while. I did them mainly for two reasons. First, I wanted to make sure these subjects were added to my students' Christian worldview. This was critical. Second, I did them when either midterms or finals were coming up, as a review. I did these two chapel talks three weeks apart.

Kids, I met a man the other day who was an avid L.A. Dodgers fan. He knew the history of the team, in Brooklyn and in L.A. He knew the great players then and now. He rattled off the names of Jackie Robinson, Roy Campanella, Pee Wee Reese, Sandy Koufax and their records, the owners, Walter O'Malley and all the managers including Leo Dresher and Walter Ashton; yesterday's greats like Kurt Gibson and today's heroes Clayton Kershaw, Justin Turner and manager, Dave Roberts. He knew all the batting averages, pitching percentages, and could even name their wives and children. I couldn't get him to shut up; he kept going and going! I finally had to say, "Hey Bob, I've got to get going, but I am very impressed with your knowledge of the team." As I walked away, I thought, "Wow, that guy really knew his team!"

It was the same when I was a flight instructor. I would often take a student to Prop-n-Wings coffee shop to go over some flight procedures. There, all the pilots would be talking about their airplanes. They knew all the makes and models, the Piper 140s, 180s, Arrows, Comanches, the Cessna 150s and 180s, the twin-engine 310s and 402s. They could rattle off the runway distances needed for landing and takeoffs, the stall speeds, cruising speeds, and top speeds for every one of these planes. They knew how much fuel they burned in an hour. They knew everything about general aviation.

I noticed the same thing when I was an Ag Consultant for equine and bovine nutrition, in the horse and cattle industry. I once was employed by a wealthy racing horse owner to plan a nutrition schedule for his stables. I went to some championship races when his horses were competing. Once, he sent a driver to pick me up, along with his agent, to take us to a championship race. As soon as I got into the limo, the agent began rattling off all the horses in the big race. He knew the horses, their breeding, the sires and dams, and their grandsires. He knew all the times they ran in the half-mile and mile. He knew all the champions fifty years back! I was thankful once I got out of the limo at home around two in the morning! I thought, "Wow! These guys really know and love their hobbies."

I was impressed with two things about these people. One, they really had knowledge about their particular interests and two, their enthusiasm and passion for these interests were a bit overwhelming. Later, when I became a Biblical Studies teacher, teaching theology and Old Testament, I would often ask my students, parents, laymen and, even once, elders in a church, "Who is God?" Most times, they would ask me what I meant by the question. I'd ask them to tell me what they knew about God. Every time, I would get answers like, "God is the one that sent Jesus Christ to die for our sins," or "God is the one that worked miracles for Moses," or "God created the world." Then I would say, "Tell me what you know about His personality!" I only got blank stares. Wow! I thought about how even Bob, Frank, and my pilot friends—frail, feeble human beings—knew more about their interests than most Christians knew about their God, who is the creator and sustainer of all life! And they had more passion!

I thought, no one will graduate from this school not knowing who their God is and not knowing about His personality. Passion, I'll leave up to the Holy Spirit to supply. However, through all my years of teaching, I have learned this truth: that getting to know who God is and His true personality, combined with a real desire to please Him, will necessarily lead you to a passion for Him and to service with Him.

So here we go, who is God? When theologians talk about this subject, they generally use the term, God's attributes, but I prefer the word character to explain who God is and His personality. When you want to inquire about a good friend's reputation, you don't want to know about his or her attributes but about their character. How honest is he? How dependable is she? And so on.

So, what is God's true character? Like Bob, Frank, and my pilot friends, all they knew about their passion they had to get from their observations or from books. Bob had to go to the stats book. Frank had to go to the record books, and my pilot friends had to go to their flight manuals to get all the specifications of their various airplanes. So, we also must go to our "flight manual," the Bible, to find out the characteristics of our creator. Our Bibles! That's the true source of facts about Him.

Theologians also divide the characteristics of God into two categories—communicable characteristics and incommunicable characteristics. Incommunicable ones are those qualities of God that we just can't comprehend, like that God is eternal, for example. We can't relate to that because we don't know anything that doesn't die or decay or eventually disintegrate. Our limited mental abilities cannot comprehend that concept so God cannot communicate this idea of Himself to us. Therefore, theologians call these the un- (or not) communicable characteristics of God.

The other communicable characteristics of God are those that we can comprehend because God makes them clear to our understanding, like God being just. We can relate to this because we know people who are just and unjust. These are characteristics we can relate to.

So, students, in the next chapel talk, I am going to go over these two categories of God's character so that when someone asks you to tell them about your God, you will not need to hesitate or have an inadequate answer. You will say, "Let me tell you how marvelous our God is."

Closing Prayer:

Oh God, forgive us when others know all about earthly things which will soon pass away and yet we do not know all about what You have revealed to us in Your Word about You, who invites us to live with You for eternity. Please give us a passion to know and love You, Christ and Your Holy Spirit and a desire to serve You with our lives. Amen.

Truth Theme: Don't be embarrassed by what you don't know about God. Get knowledge of who He is and become emboldened to explain Him to others.

coach@chapelfield.org

CHAPEL TALK
50
Who Is Your God?
(Part II)

"Immortal, invisible, God only wise, in light
inaccessible hid from our eyes, most blessed,
most glorious, the Ancient of Days, Almighty,
victorious, Thy great name we praise."

"Immortal, Invisible, God Only Wise,"
Walter C. Smith

A Thought for Today

WHO IS YOUR GOD?
(Part II)

Last week I talked to you about how discouraged I was that my Christian acquaintances knew very little about who their God really is. While most of my worldly friends knew every detail about what they loved and what their particular interests were in. So, we in the Biblical Studies department here decided that no one would graduate from this school without clearly being able to articulate who their God is and why we Christians can get so excited about our Savior. Kids, this is what we designed our comprehensive Biblical Studies program to do. This is why you will have senior comprehensive biblical exams, which will cover all of the high school Bible courses before you graduate. So, this morning I want to briefly give you another rung in your ladder of appreciation for God.

One rung in the top of the ladder is that our God is a **magnificent creator**. Equal to it is that our God is an **ingenious Savior**. The word magnificent has in its prefix the mag- meaning big or large, and the whole word refers to *great, splendor, of great importance, superb, of very great power, of awesome ability*. Our English language cannot express the magnitude of the actual overwhelming majesty and beauty of our God, but these words were the best that I could find.

However, the Bible helps us out here by telling us what the characteristics of God's personality are. In the first place, He is **eternal**. The psalmist wrote, "Your years will never end" (Psalm 102:27). And Jeremiah wrote, "He is... the everlasting King" (Jeremiah 10:10). Can you imagine anything that exists "from everlasting to everlasting" (Psalm 90:2)?

I once asked my theology class to give me an image that best represents what they think eternal looks like. One drew a railroad track, wide at the start and then merging into one continuous line. Another student said she thinks of her bed. There is no way to describe eternity. That's why kids, the theologians call this and other of His characteristics (or attributes) incommunicable, because God does not communicate them to us, for we don't have minds capable of understanding them. Wow! That's good to know because Jesus said, "They follow Me, and I give them eternal life" (Matthew10:27-28). If Jesus did not possess it, He could not give it. But He does, and He gives it freely to all who believe. That's who our God is!

The Bible also says that our God is **self-existing** (His aseity). We don't know anything that exists without help from outside itself. Humans need food, water, shelter, companionship, etc. But God needs nothing to support His existence. He said, "I am that I am" (Exodus 3:14)—I have life in and of Myself. That is our God!

The Bible goes on to say that our God is **immutable**. "For I am the Lord; I change not" (Malachi 3:6). This means He cannot just change His mind. Did you ever see a creature that doesn't change its mind? You and I go back and forth on our word every day! But God never goes back on His. That's why we can depend on God to keep His promises to us. What kind of God is that? No other religion has this kind of God!

Now, kids, for me, this God is someone to get excited about. But the scriptures do not end describing our awesome God there. The Bible also says our God is **immense**—*mag*nificent, big, vast! And He is **omnipotent**—all-powerful! "I am God Almighty" (Genesis 17:1). He is always everywhere, or **omnipresent**. King David wrote, "Where can I flee from Your presence?"

(Psalm 139:7). Our God is all-knowing, or **omniscient**, and contains all knowledge and wisdom that ever was or will be! "All wisdom and knowledge are in Him" (Romans 11:33). These are the intrinsic, personal incommunicable characteristics of your God! This is something I can get excited about. How about you?

But that is not all the Bible says about God. It also defines His external characteristics which we can understand. He communicates these and extends these to us. Since we are created in the image of God (*imago Dei*), we were created to likewise exhibit these. Our God is holy, righteous, and just. He is also good, merciful, and loving. Wow! What kind of God is this? Sovereign in all His internal characteristics and perfect in all of His external characteristics, just the God we need to live under equitably, in peace and in safety forever!

However, there is one catch. We are supposed to exhibit these external characteristics and when we do not—when we are not holy, righteous, just, good, merciful, and loving—we sin against the image of God He placed in us by failing to reflect the God that is like that. This character assassination of God is called sin, or missing the mark of the *imago Dei*. Our sin creates a debt that we owe to God, and the cost of it is our death and eternal punishment. We are hopeless. Such a great God wants everything for us, and we screw it up.

Now comes our God's **ingenious plan** and **saving power**. In a position between two opposing attributes—His righteousness and His loving compassion—God gave us the gospel. Jesus Christ paid our debt on the cross thereby uniting God's righteousness with His compassion. Thus we can have "peace with God through our Lord Jesus Christ" (Romans 5:1). We must accept God's solution through repentance and faith that Jesus truly is God and that God raised Him from the dead (Romans 10:9-10). At that point, kids, because of God's ingenious saving power, we are united to the **magnificent**, awesome, beyond-our-imagination, God that created everything in the universe!

So, that is something to desire to know all about and to get excited about. It drives the puny interest in horses back to their stables, airplanes back into their hangers and baseball into the minors. What can stand up to this magnificent and ingenious saving God? Nothing in this world! So, when someone asks you, "What do you know about your God?" tell them this story!

Closing Prayer:

Oh, our Father, please give us a clear view of who You are, thrill us with Your magnificence and love for us. Never let this knowledge slip away from us but keep it on the tips of our tongues every moment of every day. Amen.

Truth Theme: Know who your God is and, with great joy, proclaim Him to your world.

coach@chapelfield.org

CHAPEL TALK
51

Will Katy, Nathaniel, and Jaden Yet Live?

> "Look to the eternal gain of your child. Your child has attained eternal glory. Your little one is safely in the arms of God, alive forever and fully mature and like Christ."
>
> John MacArthur,
> *Safe in the Arms of God*

A Thought for Today

WILL KATY, NATHANIEL, AND JADEN YET LIVE?

Background: In 2008, I had a young teacher, Seth, who together with his wife Pamela, was expecting his first child. The baby went full-term, _but_ when the _day_ came for the delivery, the baby became entangled in the umbilical cord and died. This reminded me of how my wife (whom all students throughout the years have referred to as Mom) and I lost a baby at birth. It was especially difficult for us as, though we already had three healthy boys, this was the girl we had been hoping for. I did a chapel talk at the time of Seth and Pam's loss because we were all greatly grieved, and the students had many questions.

I have updated that chapel a bit to include relevant circumstances related to the first student I brought over from our orphanage in Africa. After living here some thirteen years, during which time he married my secretary, he and his wife, Ashley, lost their baby, Jaden, who was born prematurely at twenty-two weeks, lived for just over a month and passed away. Here is the message I gave to the students and faculty, now updated. All three families are strong Christians.

I know all of you are grieving with Seth and Pam. However, kids, we live in a cursed world. This is because we have sinned and rebelled against God's righteous standards which He has set for us. This sin has affected all the earth, people, and animals. That sin brings violence, crimes against humanity, sickness, suffering, and death to us all—humans and animals.

The good news we know is that Jesus Christ so loved this

world that He died to save us from the consequences of that sin and these horrible effects of it. He guarantees those who believe in Him that they will inherit a New Earth where these terrible effects of sin will not ever be present again. But the good news doesn't stop there. He also gives us new life here and now and guarantees both Mom and I, Seth and Pam and Joseph and Ashley that we will see Katy, and Nathaniel and Jaden again.

But you might ask, "How can that be?" These infants have not yet repented of their original sin? They had not yet confessed belief in Christ. Although all human beings are born sinful (As King David even said, "In sin did my mother conceive me."), and all babies are born crying and demanding, "pick me up, feed me," like self-centered savages, as one of my professors once described them. They are totally egocentric. They had not chosen to **willingly** sin like you and I. They simply act out of the instinct of their fallen nature. After a few years as their reasoning developed, their sinful natures would eventually lead them to willfully violate God's commands as Adam and Eve did.

Then the question is, how does God forgive infants? Simply out of His pure, loving grace, just like He did for you and me when we did not ask for His grace, nor did anything to earn it. Although, all those He has chosen to be His people will be given faith by His Holy Spirit to believe and repent of their willful and sinful behavior. John MacArthur reminds us in his great little book, *Safe in the Arms of God,* that King David said after he lost his child born to Bathsheba, "I shall go to him," (2 Samuel 12:23), being confident that he would see his child again.

Kids, there will be a lot of orphans in heaven, created by those who willfully kill their babies who bear God's image, in their womb. Those mothers who have not repented of this horrendous crime will face a horrible end in eternity. Although, these mothers who willfully participated in these acts of murder are also created in God's image, so we love them and pray for them that they will turn to Christ and ask for forgiveness while they still have life.

So, we all grieve with Seth and Pam, and Joseph and Ashley now. Jesus himself commands that we mourn with those that mourn. But I was six years old when my uncle left our family as First Lieutenant to fight the Japanese in the hot, sweltering South Pacific. For five years we waited, not knowing if at any time a Marine officer and a chaplain would be coming down our walk to bring terrible news. I had seen so many other homes in our community with black frames around the stars hanging in their windows, signifying that their sons would not be coming home. The grieving of those many mothers in our neighborhood is still vivid in my heart and mind today. But how they rejoiced when one son after another came walking down other walkways in '46 when the war was over.

Kids, there are few that stick by us when we mourn, but there will be many with us at our rejoicing when we see our loved ones again. There's a hymn that goes, "Great will be our rejoicing when Jesus we see." Why is this? First, because we will see Him face to face—our Savior, our God, our King. Then we will see our loved ones that, by His grace alone, yet live! We grieve now, but great our rejoicing will be. The apostle Paul penned these words:

> But I would not have you to be ignorant, brethren,
> concerning them which are asleep, that ye sorrow
> not, even as others which have no hope. For if we
> believe that Jesus died and rose again, even so them
> also which sleep in Jesus will God bring with him"
> (1 Thessalonians 4:13-14).

So, we mourn now but with hope and surety that we will see

these little ones again. For they yet live!

Closing Prayer:

Oh God, please be very close to Seth and Pam, and Joseph and Ashley at this time. May all Your promises come true. For we are trusting in You. Amen.

Truth Theme: You can rest assured that all in Christ, by His matchless grace, are guaranteed a glorious future way beyond our expectations and hopes.

coach@chapelfield.org

CHAPEL TALK

5²

Do You Have Confidence?

*"For the Lord shall be Thy confidence...
In the fear of the Lord is strong confidence."*

Proverbs 3:26, 14:26

A Thought for Today

Do You Have Confidence?

My text for this morning is found in Hebrews 10:35: "Cast not away therefore your confidence, which hath great recompense of reward." The Amplified Version puts it this way, "Do not therefore fling away your confidence for it carries a great and glorious compensation (payment) of reward." Note kids, the words *fearless confidence* and *glorious [payment] of reward.*

I want to tell you a short baseball story. In 1982, when my son Billy was twelve years old, I was the coach of his Little League team, the Dodgers. That year, we won the league championship, partly because we had two outstanding pitchers. Billy averaged twelve strikeouts a game, and Darius Mochi averaged fourteen. In two games, Darius, a six-foot-tall twelve-year-old, had sixteen strikeouts in one game. That meant, of the eighteen outs in a six-inning game, only two were not strikeouts. How would you like to be a coach going up against us, knowing that your team may be only allowed two hits in that game? I had great confidence as we went into the county championships since we won the quarterfinal game 8-2. This was behind Billy's pitching. Now came the semi-final, and I had Darius!

The day came. We all showed up at the park and started our warm-ups. Just before the game started, I sent Eric Pearson, our great catcher, to warm Darius up. Eric came running back to me and said, "Darius is behind the dugout crying." I immediately ran to see Darius. Sure enough, he was on his knees, crying. I said, "Darius, what's the matter? We've got the biggest game of the season!" He looked at me with tears in his eyes and said, "I'm afraid, and I have lost my confidence. I can't do it." I desperately tried to build his confidence back up by putting my arm around him and giving him words of encouragement but to no avail. He just wouldn't go to the mound.

Billy couldn't pitch two games in a row, according to league rules. So, I put in Keith Delaney. Keith was our cleanup hitter and had a very strong arm but had difficulty hitting the strike zone. We lost, 4-2. Our season was over. I remembered the words of the text for today—fearless confidence leads to great rewards. The rewards were over for our team. Darius did not have the courage to bring home the prize for us. I thought about how important confidence is.

I remember one of my great heroes, General George Patton. He plowed through Italy and Germany with his Third Army, this against great resistance from German forces and against great odds. Reporters asked him later how he did it. His three-word reply stuck with me all of my life. He said, "Audacity, audacity, audacity." Another way of saying this is brazen boldness or fearless confidence.

In that war also, our fighter pilots gained air superiority over the mighty German Luftwaffe in 1944. How did they do this? They had confidence in three things. First, they had confidence in their airplanes. They learned this from their aircraft flight manuals. They had the best fighter planes in the world (the P-51 Mustang, the P-38 Forked-tail Devil and the P-47 Thunderbolt). The flight manuals of these planes told them the capabilities and limits of these planes. Secondly, they had confidence in their training. They had the best training possible; they had combat-experienced instructors teaching them for hundreds of hours. Thirdly, they had confidence in their mission. They believed in their mission—defeat fascism and keep the world free for our God-given democracy to have the victory.

(clockwise, top left) North American P-51 Mustang, Lockheed P-38 Lightning, Republic P-47 Thunderbolt, Grumman F6F Hellcat, Vought F4U Corsair

As Christians, we can have the same confidence that can lead us to victory. We have our personal flight manual, the Holy Scriptures. This tells us our capabilities and limits. If we stay within those limits, it guarantees our success. Secondly, we can have confidence in the best training in the world and getting a good start right here in our Biblical Studies program. Take it seriously. It will help you avoid a crash. And thirdly, we have been given the greatest mission in history—to set people free, through the power of the gospel, from the consequences of their sin by accepting Jesus Christ through His atoning sacrifice He made on the cross. We ought to have audacity, for this is where our confidence is. Pray for it, and the Lord will give it to you! "For the Lord shall be your confidence, firm and strong, and keep your feet from hidden danger" (Proverbs 3:26, AMP).

Closing Prayer:

*Oh Lord, we are a weak and fearful people. For-
give us for our lack of confidence in You. Help us to
be strong and of good courage. Inspire us to Your
service. Give us confidence in Your Lordship and in
Your mission, we pray. Amen.*

Truth Theme: If you want to be confident in what you do for the Lord, it must be built on these three things: the Holy Scriptures, your training, and your cause. Go and get it; be fearless.

coach@chapelfield.org

CHAPEL TALK
53
Graduation Address

"My conscience is held captive to the word of
God. I cannot, and I will not recant anything...
Here I stand, I cannot do otherwise."

Martin Luther,
at the Diet of Worms, 1521

A Thought for Today

GRADUATION ADDRESS
2013

Background: I rarely spoke at our graduation ceremonies, *but* this year I had an excellent speaker lined up who was a professor from Nyack College (a Christian college just over an hour from our school) who had to back out at the last moment due to a family emergency. During my final chapel talks with the senior class, I would try to soften them up in the beginning with a little roasting, or as the kids call it, by dissing them about events that happened over the past year. Here are some of my recollections:

"Let me tell you some things I will miss about this class and some things I will not miss. For example, I would not miss seeing Julia driving out with a dent in the 'new' car her father bought her when she got her driver's license—a cream puff 1995 Chevy Impala. My principal even commented that the car now looked more like an accordion on wheels. And there's John (another great student and one of the best in my theology class, had two left feet and was always getting himself into problems). I won't miss watching John come to class dripping wet after falling through the ice on the school's pond after I specifically told the class not to go out on the inlet waterway because the ice was thin there. And there was Sarah, who when my principal and I saw her drive out of the parking lot, we turned our cell phones off for an hour because we were tired of getting emergency phone calls that she was in a wreck somewhere."

That's how it went, though, almost the entire class. There was always some faux pas to pick on. The classes usually roared about these disses. Then I moved on to my chapel talk. This was my graduation talk.

Seniors, this afternoon, I would like to talk to you about the most important thing our faculty would like you to take with you as you leave our school. It will make the difference as to whether you are pleasing and obedient to our Lord Jesus Christ. The question is, will you **stand**? Will you stand for the truth in your Christian life? Will you stand for the truth in the conflicts with our culture? The apostle Paul wrote, "Put on the whole armor of God that ye may be able to **stand** against the wiles of the devil in this evil day, and having done all, to **stand**." (Ephesians 6:11-14).

Bill Spanjer III,
giving commencement address, Graduation 1991

I suggest to you, kids, you are going to have to stand against three critical things: First, **other individuals**. You are going to find yourself out in a world with very different values and ethics than those you have been used to. You may have a roommate or a co-worker who thinks differently about what he or she can do—reckless alcohol consumption, experimenting with drugs, partying. Some individuals may have political and cultural ideas that are contradictory to Christian beliefs, like abortion, homosexual marriage, desecration of our flag and true democracy. When you are put under pressure to conform, what will you do? Will you fold or will you stand?

Second, you will have to stand against **groupthink**, against going with the crowd. They will be very convincing—"Everybody is doing it." "It can't be wrong if it makes you happy." "No one will find out." "The crowd will be too big to recognize me." Will you stand?

Finally, you will have to stand against **yourself**. You will oppose everything this school, your family, and your church has taught you. You don't believe me? Almost every year, I learn of a graduate who has gotten pregnant or has begun abusing drugs or alcohol, or even a former student who as just given up on their faith and has walked away from the church because they are having "intellectual" problems with the Bible. Kids, just this week I got a call from a lawyer defending a recent graduate who was coming up for sentencing on a charge for drug possession and stealing. The lawyer wanted to know the former student's behavior record during his time at our school and asked if I would give a statement. When she told me the name of the student, I almost fell off my chair in shock. He had been one of my best theological students! I could not believe it was him and even asked her to repeat the name one more time.

Kids, don't think it can't happen to you. Listen to what the apostle Paul said, "For I do that which I do not want to do and what I should do, I do not" (Romans 7:15). Stand, stand, stand. Put on the whole armor of God—truth, righteousness, the gospel, faith in Christ. Keep your eyes always on salvation and wielding every day the sword of the Spirit which is the word of God. You may not believe me now, but you will need all of these in order to stand!

The Greek word for stand is *histemi*, which the well-known scholar Simon Kistemaker once said means "stand firm, not idle." In other words, when a car is idling, you can still push it back and forth. But when you put your foot on the brake, whether it is idling or not, you cannot move it. It's firmly planted. Your friends may try drugs; you must put on your brakes. When the crowd wants you to go for choice and gay rights, put on your brakes. When you are tempted to compromise your faith, put on your brakes. Stand firm.

In closing, Seniors, identify with these people: Jacob, who stood against the angel ("I will not let you go until you bless me"); David, who stood against the wicked Philistines; Ruth, who stood against the advice of Naomi ("I will go with you"); Daniel, who stood against the heathen culture ("I will not eat the king's food"); Esther, who stood against the cruel Haman; Paul the apostle, who stood against the Ephesian mob; Augustine, who stood against the heresies of Pelagius; Martin Luther, who stood against the entire Roman Catholic religion stating, "Here I stand. I can do no other!" This is a crowd you can be proud to stand with.

Most graduation speakers have three points and a poem to leave you with, all of which is soon forgotten. I only have one word for you—**Stand**. Whatever evil suggestion comes your way, either from a friend, a crowd or your own mind, no matter who is tempting you, **stand** for Jesus Christ. Godspeed and good providence to you, Senior class.

Closing Prayer

Dear Lord, I pray that You would give this senior class the grace to stand for the truth that they have learned from their parents, their churches, and the truth of the gospel that they have been taught here at Chapel Field. I pray that You would give them the patience of Job, the courage of Joshua, the strength of David, and the sacrificial spirit of our Savior, Jesus Christ. Keep them safe in their futures and create in them an obsession for You and the ministry to which You will call each of them. We ask this in the name of our Lord and Savior, Jesus Christ. Amen.

Chapel Field Graduating Class

coach@chapelfield.org

QUOTES BY COACH:

To My Teachers, Staff, and Students:

"Don't destroy on the altar of tolerance what you gained on the anvil of character."

On Coach's door: *"No excuses will be accepted here; reasons will be strictly evaluated."*

"You never have to pray about doing the right or good thing; just do it. It has already been required of you."

"Warning: Never fall in love with your own rectitude."

"Remember, students, you are more than a test score."

"Most contemporary Christian music puts you to sleep then kills you theologically."

"Sinning is now a human right; if you speak the truth, you will get sued."

"Praise music generally is like cotton candy—sweet to the taste, but when you bite down, theologically, there's nothing there."

To a student complaining that his teacher has the wrong impression about him: *"My impressions are your reputation."*

To Teachers: *"If rules are broken with no consequences at all, there are no rules at all."*

"You're either busy being born or you're busy dying."

"When you cost more than you are worth, you're worthless."

"Don't let being civil stand in the way of being principled."

To My Coaches and Teams:

"If you are not learning and practicing, you are dying or dead."

"Character will be honored here before accomplishment."

"Manage the team that shows up, not the team you wanted to show up."

"Don't cause a loss by disciplining your team. You've only shown them that you are not a winner either."

A Reminder to Myself: *"Age is not holding me back, health is, and they're both trying to kill me."*

"It's all concentration, concentration, concentration."

To My Biblical Studies Classes:

"Be not prideful in boasting to others but have pride in your God and your Holy-Spirit-guided faithfulness to Him."

"In righteousness, God created us as His moral twin; in unrighteousness, we failed. In God's righteousness He sent His Son; in

righteousness, He is restoring us to be His moral twin again" (Based on 2 Corinthians 3:18).

"Our worship should produce a desire in us to produce worship in others."

"We are either all in or not in at all (based on Jesus's words in Matthew 12:30)."

Words of wisdom for a successful life from Coach's father, William H Spanjer, Jr.: "Profit lies not in doing what you are required to do but in what's done beyond what you are required to do (based on Luke 17:10-14)."

"Don't give God what you want to give Him in the future; give Him what you've got now."

"The most important word in the Bible only has two letters. By not obeying that little word, all theology is meaningless to you. That little word is 'IF' (Based on Romans 10:9-10; 1 John 1:9)."

"Although we honor the saints from the past, glorification is reserved for Christ alone."

"Gratitude is a sacred virtue."

"If you sacrifice and it don't hurt you, it ain't sacrifice."

"Look beyond your idols and see God; He requires that He be your only idol" (Based on Acts 17:24, 29).

"There no second place in the Trinity."

"Faith is a righteous act."

"Reformation biblical theology is like healthy food to your body—with it you will grow in energy and strength; without it, you will wither and starve. Feast on it."

"Suffering injustice is the cost of doing God's business in this evil world."

"Religion is not something you do but something you are."

"The gospel is very simple, but the theology behind it is very complex."

"If you are serious about your faith and your further service to Christ, pray now for God to give you an obsession with Jesus, His Word, and your further ministry. It will guarantee your successful servanthood."

"A Christian in America is like a remnant in Babylon."

"The greatest gift to mankind—the Incarnation;
The greatest gift to Christians—the Atonement;
All given, in love, by the Father, the Holy Spirit and
Jesus Christ alone."

CPSIA information can be obtained
at www.ICGtesting.com
Printed in the USA
BVHW072008060919

557832BV00003B/22/P